Father's Living Water 2

FATHER'S LIVING WATER 2

James O. Van Luke
and
Patsy Van Luke

Blue Ink Media Solutions

Father's Living Water 2

Copyright © 2024 by James O. Van Luke and Patsy Van Luke. All rights reserved.

No part of this publication may be reproduced, distributed, or transmitted in any form or by any means, including photocopying, recording, or other electronic or mechanical methods, without the prior written permission of the author, except in the case of brief quotations embodied in critical reviews and certain other noncommercial uses permitted by copyright law.

The contents of this work, including, but not limited to, the accuracy of events, people, and places depicted; opinions expressed; permission to use previously published materials included; and any advice given or actions advocated are solely the responsibility of the author, who assumes all liability for said work and indemnifies the publisher against any claims stemming from publication of the work.

Printed in the United States of America
ISBN 978-1-64133-914-8 (sc)
ISBN 978-1-64133-915-5 (e)
ISBN 978-1-64133-846-2 (hc)

This book is printed on acid-free paper.

Because of the dynamic nature of the Internet, any web addresses or links contained in this book may have changed since publication and may no longer be valid. The views expressed in this work are solely those of the author and do not necessarily reflect the views of the publisher, and the publisher hereby disclaims any responsibility for them.

2024.06.26

Blue Ink Media Solutions
1111B S Governors Ave
STE 7582 Dover,
DE 19904

www.blueinkmediasolutions.com

Chiefs Wisdom

From The Master to Follow In Tradition

His all will not be lost when all will remember His Cross, His Cloud His Love coming from above.

Everlasting Words of JESUS; in RED letters

Father's Living Water ✝ herapy Plus Prayer

A New Twist of Wisdom, within the Application of Faith, Works and Knowledge

Given By **GOD** in His flowing spirit

Through Utterance Unto

Free Spirits / Soul Mates

Lord **Jesus**, the mediator of this covenant; enjoyed by all in **Jesus**.

CREDITS

Wikipedia, Encyclopedia.com Sacredsemen.com

The Wholy Spirits The Holy Bible Webster's Dictionary

Matthew E. Powers/Poem Forever Living (Aloe Vera) lawsofwisdom.com

CONTENTS

Father's Living Water Therapy Plus Prayer 1
Credits 2
Contents 3
Preface 4

Focus in Tradition and Stay Focused 8
Introduction 9
Father's Living Water 11
GODs Law 22
Prophet / Seers Acts 3:19-24 24
Absence of GOD 29
Presence of GOD (Spirit Within) 30
Spirit Within 32
Chief Unifeatherrock 35
Healingtree 41
Mind's eye 45
See In Spiritual Journey 47
Proof That GOD Does Exist (Albert Einstein) 49
Fruit of the Spirit 56
GOD Loves 59
Significance of TWO 61
Free Will 64
Words 66
The Gospel According to you 68
I am that I am 70
Utterance 73
The Illusionist 118
Fine Pearl's 119
Thy Self 120
Everlasting 122
Serenity Prayer 123

Preface

LET GO

The longer you let it build up without letting go of it, the longer it will take to let go of it all. For that was yesterday and yesterdays' gone. It will not be what it was yesterday, nor will it be the same as this moment, for tomorrow is of moments not yet passed. Receiving the moment or the measure of the moment that **GOD** has *given*, or *gives now* or *ever will give* is in His purpose of and for the moment. When given a blessing or vision for it is His purpose to stay in tradition. For knowing this a blessing, for that if it should not come to pass, it builds up and becomes polluted. Let go of all that is not *a fruit of the spirit*. (Galatians 5:19-23) The *fruit of the Spirit* is **love, joy, peace, patience, kindness, goodness, faithfulness, gentleness and self-control.** Against such things there is no law.

    Ruled by influence of ***manipulative power of suggestion by them with power in the land***, brainwashing has us in a box, whether we are aware of it or not. Instead we should be seeking outside the box going with the flow of GOD's spirit within. Sometimes we do realize it pending on our state of mind. The state of mind may tell us it does not care any way. Everything **GOD** the Father has created is good, full of his blessing and spirit within. He is in you as you are of Him. Whole and complete is to use the fleshly mind to let go and connect to the flow. With **GOD** within we can let go of all of the insignificant stuff we keep holding on to taking up space and cluttering up our minds. It's so easy to allow our emotions to run wild when not seeking joyful love from Him. We should keep emotions at a low level and humble ourselves unto The Holy Spirit in tradition.

GETTING FREE

To seek is to find and to find is a gift. In the stillness of the spirit is where GOD and Love can always be found. Be still and trust Him in tradition. Let go of whatever it is that puts you inside the box instead of into the flow of the spirit outside of the box. Let it all go and wait patiently for the flow to come to you in the stillness. Letting go of consciousness allows the subconscious mind to be in control taking the soul into The Light of The Eye of The Higher Powers. GOD the Father supplies us with exactly what we need spiritually and fleshly because He knows all of us very well as He is our Creator.

Tradition is the handing down of a belief in custom or practice, to stay in remembrance of a routine continually. For humans must seek His spirit to receive His blessing. **GOD** knowing this of us requires tradition and to be self-disciplined to seek Him, in spirit of His making. *We are not to become stagnant and selfish;* we are to stay strong in His Blessings in flow of His purpose to make mark of a moment not yet passed. In keeping of tradition this action with purpose is granted to us by the spiritual moment of flowing. Penetrating vibrancies is replenishment, refreshing and *rerewarding* (Isaiah 58:8).

Tradition is the key to becoming a healing. Rejoice and enjoy with *delight* in life therefore fulfilling part of our purpose. (John 4:24) GOD *is* a Spirit: and they that worship Him must worship Him in spirit and in truth. GOD did not give us a spirit of *timidity*, but a spirit of power and love that throbs. Love is more than a feeling it's a living substance it's a given substance not to be polluted. We give thanks to Him the Father/creator for all in all. Saint Augustine summarized this when he wrote "Love GOD, and do as thou wilt".

PREFACE

Prayer: Lord show us the feeling of your love, we know you're out there, you know we are here, all of your spirits are so pretty, all of your spirits are so happy, you're so pretty; oh so happy. Spirits take us with you, *let us go and enjoy your flowing into us, into your making and feeling all the love and fullness within.* For of your spirits flowing will add into us as your making is now within us.

How do we focus? To focus is to *become aware of* and *concentrate, totally.* Let go of all other thoughts that interfere with the process of focusing. No distractions whatsoever can interfere with totally focusing. We must look at the overall picture as "ONE." We look at it as a *whole*, not in pieces/parts.

Really look at it good. If something is broken it needs repairs because it won't work. GOD's Time is our time to equal Sacrifice. We spend time with Him making His Time, ours. We are both sacrificing to do so.

Good thing and bad thing pending on who is making the choice and whether or not one is seeking and trusting **JESUS** in all things great and small every moment. If we can seek and find a little spark of Joy each day in some simple way then the love of **GOD** will surely come our way. (Matt. 6:33) Knowing His presence and experiencing His peace allows you to make decisions in life that conform to His will. When an individual practices the presence of **GOD**, that individual will have access to information. This information is available to all individuals and in that information will be found purpose of **GOD's** Free Will to control our actions as human souls He is our creator. FOCUS ON TRADITION AND REJOICE; ONLY GOOD COME'S FROM GOOD HABITS.

Now you teachers can teach, you parents can also teach your children for now you are ready to do so. Unless you are right with GOD, you can't be right. Therefore if we are going to do anything at all then *why not do it right?*

I Cor. 2:7 But we speak the wisdom of GOD in a mystery, even the hidden wisdom, which GOD ordained before the world unto our glory: **8** Which none of the princes of this world knew: for had they known it, they would not have crucified the Lord of glory. **9** But as it is written, Eye hath not seen, nor ear heard, neither have entered into the heart of man, the things which GOD hath prepared for them that love Him. **10** But GOD hath revealed them unto us by his Spirit: for the Spirit searcheth all things, yea, the deep things of GOD. **11** For what man knoweth the things of a man, save the spirit of man which is in him? even so the things of GOD knoweth no man, but the Spirit of GOD. **12** Now we have received, not the spirit of the world, but the spirit which is of GOD; that we might know the things that are freely given to us of GOD. **13** Which things also we speak, not in the words which man's wisdom teacheth, but which the Holy Ghost teacheth; comparing spiritual things with spiritual. **14** But the natural man receiveth not the things of the Spirit of GOD: for they are foolishness unto him: neither can he know them, because they are spiritually discerned. **15** But he that is spiritual judgeth all things, yet he himself is judged of no man. **16** For who hath known the mind of the Lord, that he may instruct him? But we have the mind of Christ.

Focus in Tradition and Stay Focused

"ONLY GOOD COMES FROM GOOD HABITS"

LOVE IN WORDS GIVEN BY SPIRIT

The best habit that you can have
is to trust in JESUS
Every day in all things great and small By
seeking Him tell Him that you trust Him.
Keep beauty in mind and your
vision will always be kind.

His Cloud His Love coming from above.
His all will not be lost when all
will remember His Cross

Introduction

Therefore I walk in the world of light; I will cast no shadow for the light is within me. JESUS says, "Take up your cross and follow me." He is telling us to connect our souls to His as His Cross is His glowing Flowing Soul within His cloud coming from above.

As a creator: professor to be the father/author of these words. My inspiration for writing comes from the wholly spirit. All our family and most of all (*My Wife / Soul Mate*), has also inspired me as they all have received from me as I have freely given of myself. I will continue to write and teach, giving of myself unto others as long as the wholly spirit allows. The following is a compilation of how and what I am being taught therefore I am giving of myself in sharing of His return.

Natural: What nature gives to us as beautiful, wonderful and free has become replaced with many illusions or deceptions causing more problems than solutions. By tradition our ancestors could cure themselves of disease. They knew how to use their healing powers or natural remedies to cure diseases. There is something natural and free that exists somewhere in the world as a cure for all diseases. A solution to every existing problem can be found somewhere out there.

Meditation is the best medicine for the mind as it can bring healing powers. To seek is to find and to find is a gift. In the stillness of the spirit is where GOD and Love can always be found. Be still and trust Him. Let go of whatever it is that puts you inside the box instead of into the flow of the spirit outside of the box. Let it all go and wait patiently for the flow to come to you in the stillness.

Ruled by influence of *manipulative power of suggestion*, brainwashing has us in a box, whether we are aware of it or not.

Instead we should be thinking outside the box going with the flow of the spirit within. Sometimes we do realize it pending on our state of mind. The state of mind may tell us it does not care any way. Everything **GOD** the Father has created is good, full of his blessing and spirit within. He is in you as you are of Him. Whole and complete is to use the fleshly mind to let go and connect to the flow found in our subconscious mind.

Natural or supernatural medicines are any substance used as a remedy in treating disease, preventive, curing and improving with preserving health. There are natural spirit enhancers coming from nature when used wisely and correctly can increase our chances of finding our true destinies. Therefore everything **GOD** the Father has created is good, full of His blessing and spirit within and has a definite purpose.

Father's Living Water

JESUS said: John7: 37 In the last day, that great *day* of the feast, JESUS stood and cried, saying, If any man thirst, let him come unto me, and drink. [38] He that believeth on me, as the scripture hath said, out of his belly shall flow rivers of living water.

Psalm 23: He makes me lie down in green pastures: he leadeth me beside still waters.

(Genesis 1) The Holy Spirit is From GOD. Where it is written that "the spirit of **GOD** was floating over the waters of creation" He saw it was good (living water)

Living Water: If you have ice (solid form) it's still living water; if you have steam (gas form) it's still living water; if you have water (liquid form) it's still living water and it's components did not change just the form. The same is true of the Holy Trinity, **GOD** the Father, **GOD** the Son and **GOD** the spirit. No matter how you *shape it*, or where *it comes from*, or what *contains it*, or what is *contained within it*, or what of its *purpose of flowing*, it's still living water. Everything **GOD** has created is good and all relative by spirit of life within water for without spirit within the Fathers living water of life with flow there will be no life.

SAP is living water the juice that circulates through a plant, tree, animal or human bearing living water, with food etc. liquid considered vital to the life or health of any organism for humans to drink indeed of as food to nourish and replenish.

Milk is living water the juice that is in a plant or human or fruits bearing living water. That is a white or yellowish liquid or any various liquid for humans to drink of as food to nourish.

Wine is living water the juice that is in a plant or fruits bearing living water. That is a liquid or any various liquid, for humans to drink of as food and lift up spirit.

Cloud's in the sky when ready, to His purpose as nature not of free will they give of them self from within, power and spirit for our lives living water, from within to drink of, for our replenishment, and to water gardens everywhere.

Medicine is living water any various liquid, for humans to drink of as natural or supernatural power, a substance used as a remedy in treating disease, preventive, curing and improving with preserving health. It is filled with goodness, power that throbs with spirit within. Spirit in liquid is food for the soul. (as drink indeed)

Earth: Our planet of life has 70% (Approx.) water over land. Humans are composed of 93 % (Approx.) water. Science says that where there is water there can be life within the living water. Humans are conceived by living water, nurtured, drink of milk and living water, cleaned, swim and baptized and laid to rest in water. Have songs "The Sea of love". You will die if you don't drink of it (dry bones). We do not live without living water within. Yet only 3% (Approx.) on the planet is drinkable by humans.

To Seek is To Meditate: First I find the **GOD** given spirit within the flesh (soul) therefore all of the good shall be in the flesh according to His purpose. We human's are in the kingdom of **GOD** filled with his spirit in the flesh, with different callings of his purpose to His will. Humans are of free spirit to do His called purpose in the flesh, of them that love His spirit and His laws. We walk in His spirit and in His law then his purpose is Complete. **GOD** requires tradition of His kingdom to His purpose. This needing action of worship, this action will remind His human kingdom (Souls) that He is Lord of heaven and earth. 1Corin.13 All **GOD** the Father created is good and full of blessing in His Charity.

Humans only by free will take measure of **GODs** word that is not His purpose, for only **GOD** is to measure of human. The rest of His kingdom must receive of His purpose by nature therefore are not of free will or free spirit. Humans must seek His spirit to receive His blessing. **GOD** knowing this of us requires tradition to be self-disciplined to seek Him, in spirit of His making. *For when you receive you will believe and when you believe that you receive* therefore achieving His Blessing full of spiritual gifts of life and His love.

Spiritual Moment: Humans are **GODs** moment collectors. How long is a moment or its measure?

There is a moment that we humans are all of **GODs** collectors of His moments. To those that receive the moment or the measure of the moment in His spirit in His charity that He has given, or gives now or ever will give is in His purpose of and for the moment. For what is a moment without **GODs** blessings or His spirit within a moment that He has made. For of this moment what is the measure, from the beginning to the end? There are moments for remembering and to treasure as there are moments to let go of and forget. Ask the Wholly spirit to show you the difference. *For the moment does not move as all passes through it in the stillness of the moment.* The only thing moving in the moment is the Spiritual Journey. Of moments passed I worked for a living, now I live for **GOD** working moments in me. To receive a moment of **GOD** charity that He has given is a blessing for only He can take them away. By letting go of our consciousness we are submitting all that we are unto Him as He ever so humbly in our subconscious mind gives spiritual gifts so abundantly. All that breathes the air is with spirit therefore having a moment of and in Fathers creation.

Flock: Like sheep following in a flock, humans are in a flock of His making. As the good shepherd goes so do the flock. **GOD** the Father created mother earth and nature, of this we are all made by and of the same that is of His making. When the good shepherd gives us a law, dream, vision, calling, purpose or blessing of His charity we humans of our free will are to follow the good shepherd with devotion in tradition to His purpose.

Human: 1Corin.11:3 It is written in the Bible, that humans are required to follow as tradition, that a wife be obedient to her husband, and in *his return* of this, he love her body as his own. For when a man gives from his body with spirit, into her body from his body, then she is of his body in this spirit. For of this action they become as one body (soul mates) (Oneness) of this spirit. Husband, submits to **GOD** and thy wife submits to her husband.

Relative: Prov.18:4 Therefore **GOD** knows His spirit of love grows when His living water flows. That is why we are called ONE of the same. The body is one of flowing spirit in the flesh, with different purpose, all made from star (light of past) dust. For what is flesh without spirit of life within? From dust we came to dust we return. We do not live without flowing living water added into the dust. Einstein (ref.)"$E=MC^2$"argument of theory: **Energy** is flowing spirit, **Mass** is flesh and **GOD** is the light. (Relativity **E=MG**)

Measure: Psalm 23 I say to you if my cup is full, for it is of my understanding of the amount of my cup. If you say to me your cup is full, for it is still my understanding the amount of my cup. For what is the amount of a cup to the understanding of each their own amount that is required to fill the cup. For I ask of you what is the measure of amount required to fill each cup? For my cup will not be full, to your amount for your cup will run over from my amount. For I ask what is the measure of the amount to fill a cup? When I give into you my full cup or all of its measure it is of my understanding not yours. For what is the amount or measure in understanding of a full cup? Selah

Treasure: Prov. 3:13 You may not have understanding or knowledge or the knowledge of the understanding. For when you have understanding of the knowledge then you become *aware* you have intelligence or wisdom which is the application of knowledge. For of this **GOD** given gift in measure from Him you are a treasure to Him, in His spirit in the flesh of His purpose. When you receive knowing it to be true, for of this you are blessed.

Human Spirit: We are human beings going through a temporary spiritual experience as we are also spiritual beings going through a temporary human experience.

Heaven: Matt. 18:18 All we hold true or worship or bind on earth so will it be bound in heaven. For what we hold not to be true or reject or loose on earth so it will be in heaven. As for me I bind all **GOD** given spirit He grants to me. For of this action of purpose is heaven on earth in the flesh. For when you *believe you will receive* His blessings, miracles, goodness and power from His spirit. As for me I refuse to reject of His blessings to me therefore I seek them and pray to Him to grant them to me and hold in remembrance. For of this I can share, teach and give of this unto others. I yearn for every spiritual moment that **GOD** grants to me. Matt.6:9 The **Lord's** Prayer "His Will be done on earth as it is in heaven".

Channeling: By detaching yourself from all matter the sub conscious mind is now controlling the conscious mind therefore you have enabled The Wholly (Holy) Spirit to work in you. Channeling is meditation which simply allows this Source of Power there for you at all times to come into yourself to filter your mind. They are always there for us but through so many distractions we have a tendency to ignore them instead of connecting unto them as should be. **GOD** supplies us with exactly what we need spiritually and fleshly because He knows all of us very well as He is our soul creator.

On a television news broadcast not so long ago a guy had been spotted on the beach and overheard by spectators to be saying he was as **GOD** the Father. Misunderstood, ridiculed, criticized and looked down upon is how we are seen by those who refuse to see and listen. Because of our brainwashed society spreading it all around the Majority is the major influence. Therefore major influence rules the majority yet will not influence those who are in the Minority who know the differences of good and bad influence "Thank **GOD**." Filtering the mind is a function and a wonderful gift to behold recognized as a blessing and a *rereward*.Isaiah52:12 Therefore "Them that know "KNOW".

Flow: Keep the spirit moving and the spirit will move us. **GOD** does not want us to spoil anything or let anything spoil. If we receive but do not give, we are causing a spoil and pollution to happen because the flow has ceased therefore becoming stagnant and selfish. For in life living water flows up. What goes up must come down and vs. versa. In nature there is a root that comes from the seed that was planted and nurtured. The living water goes into the ground to enter into the root which takes the living water up to the stem to release the living water upward into the leaf.

Prepare: As a man (soul mate) I am to prepare my place within my center. I am committed to stay strong in spirit and give into you of His making, this glorious living water/creator that **GOD** grants to me. For to me in tradition every flowing spiritual moment of His giving is glorious, for it is **GOD** who has made this living water thy creator within me to continue into her, for her to be replenished.

Prepare: As a female (soul mate) I am to prepare my place within my center. I am committed to stay in strong spirit and receive into me of His/his making, this glorious living water that **GOD** grants for me. For to me in tradition every flowing spiritual moment of His giving is glorious, for it is **GOD** who has made this living water/creator to continue into me from Him/him to replenish me.

Powers: The Powers that throb being received know of whatever want and need may be. There all of the time; here, always near; out of sight out of mind yet *insight in mind* is truly where we want them to be consciously and sub consciously. One may be under a mild state of hypnosis sub consciously and still be conscious even though being controlled by the sub conscious mind. In Prophecy is the same function of the mind. The spirit can be found in the sub conscious mind that contains nothing of the conscious mind.

Love god: Human male/soul mate, a shepherd in thee there be, every spiritual moment, out of sight out of mind. *Insight in mind* is truly where I want to be. **GOD** given spirit of powers received to know of the want and need for her within me.

Love godess: Human female/soul mate, I am in thee they are there every spiritual moment, out of sight out of mind. *Insight in mind* is truly where I want to be. **GOD** given spirit of powers that I receive lets Him/him my shepherd know of what I want and what I need, to be replenished by His/his Love into me.

Replenished: To make full or complete again, to receive as by a new supply of good and power to resupply again. It is a blessing to receive the spirit that is of **GODs** making of His Love; Charity in giving of spiritual and worldly gifts.

Tradition: The handing down of a belief in custom or practice, to stay in remembrance of a routine continually. For humans must seek His spirit to receive His blessing. **GOD** knowing this of us requires tradition and is why He requires us to be self-disciplined to seek Him, in spirit of His making. We are not to become stagnant and selfish we are to stay in His Blessings in flow of His Purpose to make mark of a moment not yet passed with measure. In Keeping of tradition this action with purpose is granted to us by the spiritual moment of flowing. Penetrating vibrancies is your replenishment, refreshing and *rerewarding* Isaiah 58:8: to pass in passing through the moment that is ours. With remembrance of the spirit that gives to us the flow, we give thanks in return, fulfilling this purpose. Kept strong in tradition only good will come, from good habits as with seeking GOD only good comes from Him thy creator.

Tradition: 1 day (sunrise to sunrise) Enjoy, flowing spirit of delight twice a week (approx.) 52 weeks per 1 year or (1complete trip around the sun).

Habits To Do: Every day (sunrise to sunrise) of 365 days or 1 year or (1complete trip around the sun). ENJOY LIFE in tradition, fulfilling His purpose. Enjoy the joy in me. Enjoy the joy in you. Enjoy Him in me. Enjoy flowing spirit, with flow. Enjoy the flowing into me. Enjoy all spiritual moments. (In Application of Faith)

Words: A spirit of love is in the words that are in this letter, given to me his servant for our fulfillment. For without the words there can be no letter. For our love in words is given by spirit. *What do these words say to you?* Words are not what they say without spirit of your understanding of the spirit in the words. The spirit has only your understanding of the words given by the spirit.

Believe: It's not about having to do something risky, it's about having the courage to do what is right and true. It's not about running in the dark it's about walking in the light. It's not about what people say, it's about believing what **GOD** says to you is right.

Light: For as I walk in this world of light I will cast no shadow, for **GODs** delight be in me. A bright candle of habit I will be, day by day, delight to delight. In delight in mind is truly where I want to be, with His delight showing the way of good habits and tradition.

Free Will: Good thing and bad thing pending on who is making the choice and whether or not one is seeking and trusting **JESUS** in all things great and small every moment .If we can seek and find a little spark of Joy each day in some simple way then the love of **GOD** will surely come our way Matt. 6:33. Knowing His presence and experiencing His peace allows me to make decisions in my life that conform to His will. When an individual soul practices the presence of **GOD**, that individual will have access to information. This information is available to all individual souls and in that information will be found purpose of **GODs** Free Will to control our actions as human and divine souls of His grace.

Full Circle: What goes up must come down and vs. versa. Recycling is replenishing and has fulfilled a purpose. When the rays from the sun absorb the water from the earth it is being filtered by the sun as it is taken into the atmosphere. For life; in life living water flows up. In nature there is a root that comes from the seed that was planted and nurtured by living water. The living water goes into the ground to enter into the root which takes the living water to the stem to release the living water upward into the leaf. From that point on a bud forms to blossom therefore patiently waiting to be pollinated. If it is not pollinated it has a different purpose altogether and goes no further. Instead the bloom from the bud falls off and no fruit has formed to reproduce the purpose of the plant. The blossom not being pollinated falls to the ground defeating the purpose to produce to therefore replenish the soil. It has a new purpose as compost replacing the purpose to reproduce.

In the female human adult eggs are dropped for the purpose of becoming fertilized by the male sperm. If not fertilized the purpose has changed altogether. With the blood flow of menstruation the egg moves on to defeat the original purpose to end up in a recycling process of replenishment as a new purpose.

Everything has spirit and with spirit comes purpose. To complete the purpose is to act upon it. To defy the purpose is to waste it. Moments come with purpose and purpose comes with the flowing within that moment.

Waste not Want not: In the winter time our family had a full barrel of good fruit, some would start to spoil, we eat the spoiled first so they would not spoil the rest not yet spoiled. In doing so we ate spoiled fruit all winter long, wasting all the good of the barrel all winter long, never enjoying of the good. For us not enjoying of the good, we are wasting and spoiling fresh living water from within His fruit.

(His creation of sweet fruit)

Love In The Words Given By Spirit.

The best habit that you can have is to trust in JESUS.

Every day in all things great and small by seeking Him tell Him that you trust Him. Keep beauty in mind and your vision will always be kind as beauty likewise keeps you in mind therefore all being good. Even though words are useless in the spirit world we must use them in the fleshly world. The Spirit feels as the flesh receives the feelings thus putting them into words thereafter.

The good spirits are just here never ending, never forceful and always helpful to those who seek them and know how to find them.

Anticipate nothing at all, wait patiently and all good shall come our way in the flow of His Blessings as we trust Him in all things great and small. AMEN, Selah

Summary: For it is necessary to us for us and of us to give of ourselves unto one another in spirit and flesh to satisfy tradition. Therefore no pollution, spoil on stagnant living water exists. The flow of the spirit must go on as within the flesh.

GODs Law

Ten Commandments: Exodus 20 (**Old Covenant**)

1-Thou shalt not have no other GODs before me.
2-Thou shalt not make unto thee any graven image.
3-Thou shalt not bow down thyself to them, nor serve them: for I the Lord thy GOD am a jealous GOD.
4-Thou shalt not take the name of the Lord thy GOD in vain.
5-Remember the Sabbath day, to keep it holy.
6-Honor thy father and thy mother: that thy days may be long upon the land which the Lord thy GOD giveth thee.
7-Thou shalt not kill.
8-Thou shalt not commit adultery.
9-Thou shalt not steal.
10-Thou shalt not bear false witness against thy neighbor, Thou shalt not covet thy neighbors house, thou shalt not covet thy neighbors wife, nor his manservant, nor his maidservant, nor his ox, nor his ass, nor any thing that is thy neighbors.

(New Covenant) through JESUS Christ

Commandments given in the Decalogue and the eternal principles upon which the Mosaic Covenant was founded still apply to those under the New Covenant, **GOD**'s people are now totally free from the Old Covenant as a covenant; that the usefulness of the Mosaic commands is not therefore to be denied, only that these are now understood to come to us through Christ, the mediator of the New Covenant; its relevance now pointing to that rest enjoyed by all those in Christ.
(Ref.) wikipedia.org/

Mark 12: 29 And JESUS answered him, The first of all the commandments is, Hear, O Israel; The Lord our GOD is one Lord: **30** And thou shalt love the Lord thy GOD with all thy heart, and with all thy soul, and with all thy mind, and with all thy strength: this is the first commandment. **31** And the second is like, namely this, Thou shalt love thy neighbour as thyself. There is none other commandment greater than these.

Prophet / Seers Acts 3:19-24

In Christianity, they are often referred to as "seers" according to 1 Samuel 9:9. Christians share the belief that a prophet is a person who speaks for GOD, in the name of GOD, and who carries GOD's message to others. Some Christian denominations teach that a person who receives a personal message not intended for the body of believers (where such an event is credited at all) should not be termed a prophet. The reception of a message is termed revelation; the delivery of the message is termed prophecy. For Christians the authenticity of a prophet is judged as JESUS said; that one should judge a prophet, by his fruits. (Gospel of Matthew 7: 15-20) (Deuteronomy 18:21-22)

Christians recognize that anyone they consider prophetic is still human and fallible, and may make wrong decisions, have incorrect personal beliefs or opinions, and sin from time to time; the human characteristics of a prophet are independent of the message GOD has given him and do not negate the validity of His prophecies.

New Testament passages that explicitly discuss prophets existing after the death and resurrection of Christ include Revelation 11:10, Matthew 10:40-41 & 23:34, John 13:20 & 15:20, and Acts 11:25-30, 13:1 & 15:32. Christians believe that the Holy Spirit leads people to faith in JESUS and gives them the ability to lead a Christian life and to give gifts (i.e. abilities) to Christians. These may include the charismatic gifts such as prophecy, tongues, healing, and knowledge. Christians holding a view known as cessationism believe these gifts were given only in New Testament times and ceased after the last apostle died. Historical records, however, contradict this theory. Christians almost universally agree that "spiritual gifts" such as the gifts of ministry, teaching, giving, leadership, and mercy (see, e.g. Romans 12:6-8) are still in effect today.

Some Christians also believe that the title "prophet" encompasses others than those who receive visions from GOD. A more modern definition of prophet is someone who spreads GOD's truths. These can be revealed in a number of ways not only visions.

(Galatians 5:19-23) **The fruit of the Spirit** is *love, joy, peace, patience, kindness, goodness, faithfulness, gentleness and self-control.*

Commonly listed gifts:
Gifts of the spirit are clearly distinguished from the fruit of the spirit (Galatians 5:22). JESUS predicted the occurrence of false gifts, particularly in the end time (Matthew 24:24, 7:22-23). Hence while spiritual gifts are very important for a Christian, the fruit of the spirit is a better test of the genuineness of a person.

Apostle: One sent by GOD with a holy mission to fulfill; and the supernatural power and spiritual gifts to fulfill the mission. One is known by his fruit of the spirit overflowing. Apostolic ministry involves laying foundation. In the case of Paul and Barnabas, we see this expressed in 'church planting' by preaching the Gospel in new areas. Apostles in scripture worked in teams. An apostolic team shared a 'measure of rule' in churches started through their ministry in regions where they are the first to proclaim the Gospel of Christ. (II Corinthians 10.)

Disciple: The term disciple is derived from the New Testament Greek word . Coming to english by way of the Latin discipulus meaning "a learner". Disciple should not be confused with *Apostle*, meaning ""messenger, he that is sent"". While a disciple is one who learns from a teacher, a student, an apostle is sent to deliver those teachings to others. The word disciple appears two hundred and thirty two times in the four gospels and the Book of Acts.

A definition for who is a disciple is JESUS' self-referential example from the Gospel of (John 13:34-35) "I give you a new commandment, that you love one another. Just as I have loved you, you also should love one another. By this everyone will know that you are my disciples, if you have love for one another."

Prophet: One who speaks, or communicates a message of authority as moved by the Holy Ghost also known by their good fruit.

Evangelist: Someone who desires that all should come to know the truth that GOD loves everyone so much that He sent His Son JESUS Christ to die for their redemption, or someone who is gifted to proclaim this message.

Pastor: A word that means 'shepherd.' Pastors are gifted to lead, guide, and set an example for other Christians.

Teacher: Someone able to understand the more difficult things of GOD and explain them in a way that is easy to understand and live by in daily life.

Servant: Supernatural ability to do for others whatever needs to be done; Divine ability to carry another burden or task without notice or earthly reward.

Exhortation: the ability to motivate Christians to do the works of Christ.

Giving: being blessed by GOD with resources or time and being able to give them where and when they are needed with a cheerful heart.

Leadership: GOD-given insight into when something needs to be done, who can do it, how it can be completed, and how to lead those people to get it accomplished.

Mercy: A heart to care for and encourage those who are not able to care for themselves and whom no one else would care for therefore knowing who to help and when to help.

Word of wisdom: A message, concept, or bit of wisdom that GOD reveals supernaturally to the recipient. It may or may not be shared with others.

Word of knowledge: A message, concept, or bit of knowledge that GOD reveals supernaturally to the recipient. It may or may not be shared with others.

Tongues: First use is a supernatural ability to speak another language not known by the believer speaking it. Second use is a supernatural ability to speak another language not known by the believer speaking it; to build up the body of Christ when the message is interpreted. It is the language of the Holy Spirit.

Interpretation of tongues: Supernatural ability to make tongues a clear message to all that are present to edify, exhort and comfort the body of Christ.

Prophecy: Supernatural ability to receive a message from GOD to edify, exhort and comfort the body of Christ or a believer. To speak as moved by the Holy Spirit as not all prophecies contain predictions about the future.

Miracle Worker: Having the ability to perform supernatural acts by the Spirit of GOD.

Gifts of healing: Supernatural ability to bring or release healing to a person in their body or soul. **Ability to distinguish between spirits**: Supernatural ability to know what is from GOD and what is not from GOD; (Divine ability to reveal a demonic spirit or influence and bring GOD's power and GOD's love in its place.)

Faith: (See Hebrews 11): Knowing what you hope for, having a conviction about things you cannot see, trusting GOD, believing GOD's Word, and obeying Him.
(Ref) wikipedia.org/wiki/Prophet

When you think of the words for example: "Can't *see* the forest for the trees." This simply means that you are looking at something but not truly seeing what you are looking at.

The Key to *seeing* and not just looking is to have the *Spirit within your* seeing the something you are looking at. It will be seen in a state of absolute reality instead of a mere illusion of reality.

The sub conscious mind must be the leader of the mind's thinking in order to see clearly. This process is including the mind's eye and the instincts that are found in all sub consciousness. For Example: "There's more there than what meets the eye."

ABSENCE OF GOD

Point of argument, that there is life and then there's death; a good **GOD** and a bad **GOD**. You are viewing the concept of **GOD** as something finite, something we can measure. To view death as the opposite of life is to be ignorant of the fact that death cannot exist as a substantive thing. Death is not the opposite of life, just the *absence* of life.

You can have lots of heat, even more heat, super-heat, mega-heat, unlimited heat, white heat, a little heat or no heat, but we don't have anything called 'cold'. We can hit up to 458 degrees below zero, which is no heat, but we can't go any further after that. There is no such thing as cold; otherwise we would be able to go colder than the lowest -458 degrees. Everybody or object is susceptible to study when it has or transmits energy, and heat is what makes a body or matter have or transmit energy. Cold is only a word we use to describe the absence of heat. We cannot measure cold. Heat we can measure in thermal units because heat is energy. Cold is not the opposite of heat, just the *absence* of heat and slows down the heating process.

Darkness is not something it is the absence of something. You can have low light, normal light, bright light, flashing light, but if you have no light constantly you have nothing and it's called darkness. That's the meaning we use to define the word. In reality, darkness isn't dark but is the absence of light.

Evil exist, at least not unto itself. Evil is simply the absence of GOD. It is just like darkness and cold, a word that man has created to describe the absence of GOD. Evil is the result of what happens when one does not have GOD's love present in his or her heart (soul). Sometimes we hear it being said as cold hearted. It's like the cold that comes when there is no heat, the darkness that comes when there is no light it's the absence of GOD. (Ref) wikipedia

Presence of GOD
(Spirit Within)

Deuteronomy 12:6 There in the **presence** of the LORD your **GOD**, you and your families shall eat, drink and shall rejoice in everything you have put your hand to, because the LORD your **GOD** has blessed you.

Psalm 61:6 May he be enthroned in **GOD**'s **presence** forever; appoint your *love* and faithfulness to protect Him.

Heb.2:14 Forasmuch then as the children are partakers of flesh and blood, He also Himself likewise took part of the same; that through death He might destroy him that had the power of death, that is, the devil; For in Him dwelleth all the fullness of the Godhead bodily.

Acts 17:24 **GOD** that made the world and all things therein, seeing that He is Lord of heaven and earth, dwelleth not in temples made with hands.

John 1:5 This then is the message which we have heard of Him, and declare unto you, that **GOD** is light, and in Him is no darkness at all.

John 4:8 He that loveth not knoweth not **GOD**; for **GOD** is *love*.

John 4:24-28 **GOD** is a Spirit: and they that worship Him must worship Him in spirit and in truth.
25 Neither is worshipped with men's hands, as though He needed anything, seeing He giveth to all life, and breath, and all things.

26 And hath made of one blood all nations of men (Souls) for to dwell on all the face of the earth, and hath determined the times before appointed, and the bounds of their habitation.
27 That they should seek the Lord, if haply they might feel after Him, and find Him, though He be not far from every one of us. (He is within you)
28 For in Him we live, and move, and have our being; as certain also of your own poets have said, For we are also His offspring. (Oneness)(His creation)(Creator)

GOD the Father that made the world and all things therein, seeing that He is **Lord** of heaven and earth. He giveth to all life, guide us continually and we will be filled with His goodness, love, joy and peace in abundance. (The Creator)

Spirit Within

Individuals who had achieved this state of being were called 'the Spiritualized', having received the 'indwelling' of the Holy Spirit through uniting with love as described in the book of Acts. (The term 'indwelling' is also used in the Kabbalah as a translation of Shekhinah, or the Glory of GOD, which is seen to dwell within the human soul.) Such individuals saw themselves as having evolved beyond ordinary states of good and evil (duality), replacing notions of faith and hope (beliefs in things which might be) with the positive light of knowledge (Gnosis, or direct knowledge of GOD the Father). (Ref) wikipedia

(Romans 11:36)(Romans 1:13)
"All things are from Him, through Him and in Him."

Luke 17:20-21
And when he was demanded of the Pharisees, when the kingdom of GOD should come, JESUS answered them and said; The Kingdom of GOD cometh not with observation: Neither shall they say, Lo, here! or, lo there! for behold, the kingdom of GOD is within you.

First Epistle of John 3: Beloved, let us love one another, for love cometh of GOD. And every one that loveth, is born of GOD, and knoweth GOD. He that loveth not knoweth not GOD; for GOD is love... If we love one another, GOD dwelleth in us, and His love is made perfect in us. Hereby know we that we dwell in Him, and He in us, because He hath given of his spirit... Whoesoever confesseth that JESUS is the son of GOD, in Him dwelleth GOD and he in GOD... For Him is love, and He that dwelleth in love dwelleth in GOD and GOD in Him For as He is, even so are we in this world"
(Acts 17:24-28)(Romans 13:1)

"GOD that made the world and all things therein, seeing that He is Lord of Heaven and Earth, dwelleth not in temples made with hands; neither is worshipped with men's hands, as though He needeth anything, seeing He giveth to all life, and breath, and all things; and hath made of one blood all nations of men for to dwell on all the face of the earth, and hath determined the times before appointed, and the bounds of their habitation; that they should seek the Lord, if haply they might feel after Him, and find Him, though He be not far from any of us; for in Him we live, and move and have our being; as certain of your poets have said, for we are also His offspring" (created by His /his living water from within the Godhead bodily)

Far

For I ask of you what is the measure of amount required to be far? For what is the measure in understanding of far to spirit? For of this moment what is the distance from the beginning to the end? Find the **GOD** given *spirit within* the flesh and all of the good is in the flesh. Therefore the spirit is inside of you without distance too far, all are one of *spirit within*. (Oneness) (Jeremiah 31:33)(Romans 13:1)

But this is the covenant that I will make with the house of Israel after those days, declares the Lord: I will put my law *within them*, and I will write it on their hearts.

I Corinthians 2:10-11:
10 But GOD hath revealed them unto us by his Spirit: for the Spirit searcheth all things, yea, the deep things of GOD.
11 For what man knoweth the things of a man, save the spirit of man which is in him? even so the things of GOD knoweth no man, but the Spirit of GOD.

Psalm 51:10-12
10 Create in me a clean heart, O GOD; and renew a right *spirit within* me.
11 Cast me not away from thy presence; and take not thy holy spirit from me.
12 Restore unto me the joy of thy salvation; and uphold me with thy *free spirit*.

Job 32:18: For I am full of matter, the *spirit within* me constraineth me.
(The need to let go, of thy flowing substance (salvation) from within)

Chief Unifeatherrock

In oneness; emanating a *gift* from GOD of whom all blessing flow. (I come, to be-come known) (Fountain of Youth in *Love*)

Chief: Being at the head first; leading; a principal leader.

Acts 14:12 And they called Barnabas, Jupiter; and Paul, Mercurius, because he was the *chief* speaker.

Acts 28:7 In the same quarters were possessions of the *chief* man of the island, whose name was Publius; who received us, and lodged us three days courteously.

Luke 22:26 But ye shall not be so: but he that is greatest among you let him be as the younger; and he that is chief, as he that doth serve.

Romans 3:2- Much every way: *chiefly*, because that unto them were committed the oracles of GOD.

(Rock) Numbers 20:8"Speak to the rock and it will emanate His/his living water. You will bring out of the rock flowing living water to drink." (as drink indeed)

Oracle: Is a person or agency considered to be a *source* of wise counsel or prophetic opinion; an infallible authority, usually spiritual in nature.

Feather: Covering of birds; projection to fit into another; to turn over water.

What, then, is a feather? It is a part of a bird's body, and it is a part of us. It exists for itself, to serve its primary purpose in the cosmos, and it exists in alliance with every other aspect of the cosmos. Just as we bring life- inspiring messages for others while simply fulfilling our own lives, so do feathers bring their messages to us. They remind us that we walk in a world overflowing with meaning.

Psalm 91:4 He will cover you with his *feather*s, and under his wings you will find refuge; his faithfulness will be your shield and rampart.

Father: Thy creator; a name given to GOD; to profess to be the author of the word.

Bliss: Blessedness; perfect *happiness*.

Blessing: GODsend; benefit; approval.

Uni: #1, One or first, of Oneness with GOD.

Younger: Youth

Dance: A ceremony as an activity, infused with significance, performed on special occasions within tradition (*dance of life*).

Flow: To transfer from one's own possession to that of another. This giving/receiving of flow is an honor.

Happiness / Blessings/Bliss (*Rejoice*): In mystical traditions, especially in advanced spiritual techniques, are related to full balance (conjunction, union, "secret marriage") of inner energy lines (energy channels of a soul or deepest dimension of the human). Positive emotions about the present are divided into two categories: pleasure and gratifications. The bodily and higher pleasures are "pleasures of the moment" and usually involve some external stimulus (*Spiritual energy*).

Water: All known forms of life depend on water. Water is vital as an essential part of many processes within the human body of flesh (*living water*).

Fountain: Obtains their water from unseen reservoir *source* that must be filled at the start from a local supply original source; a spring or source of water; the head of a river. (Source of Living Water) (his godhead bodily)

Proverbs 5:15 Drink waters out of thine own cistern, and running waters out of thine own well. [16] Let thy fountains be dispersed abroad, and rivers of waters in the streets. [17] Let them be only thine own, and not strangers' with thee. [18] Let thy *fountain be blessed*: and *rejoice with the wife* of thy youth. [19] *Let her be as* the loving hind and pleasant roe; let her breasts satisfy thee at all times; and be thou ravished always with her love.

Rev. 21: I will give unto him that is athirst of the fountain of the water of life freely. (Source of Living Water) (thy godhead bodily)

Spirit: one of the seven synonyms for GOD. These are: (fruit of the Spirit) (Galatians 5:19-23)

Fruit: *fruit of his loins* the seed that produce good offspring.

Energy: The existence of subtle, spiritual energy was well known to the ancient traditions. Most native traditions focus on the natural energies of the body for various types of healing known as *"Prana."* The energies are also used for shamanic journeys and other "acts of healing power". Common to all of the traditions is the idea that this energy has centers, or points of congregation, at various places on or near the body. The most common term for these energy centers is "chakras". Chakra is a Sanskrit word which means "vortex of energy". The number of energy centers which are identified as important varies somewhat from tradition to tradition. The feeling energy "called the water element" suffers the most.

Our excess fire has burned up our water. We are burned out, with little or no feelings (Dry Bones). From the native view our society is an emotional desert. We are out of touch with our deep feelings. We need living water added within. We need to let ourselves go in the deep living waters of life.

Inner silence is the key to tuning the energies and integrating the conscious states. It is the sacred dimension or pure awareness which unifies the otherwise unconnected states of consciousness. It is also the black hole source of the chakras. Thus all progress in spiritual disciplines depends upon reaching and retaining this inner silence. *Prima* Sounds is one way to bring you to the place of deep inner silence. (Ref) lawsofwisdom.com/Laws of Wisdom

Spiritual energy

Turn to those who you love to help you through difficult times. Draw on their spiritual energy and ask how they stay focused on their own spiritual path. Many times people we think are weak turn out to be our best source of inspiration during difficult times. When you draw spiritual energy from others, it's a boost for not only you, but them as well (Oneness). They feel better just from helping you.

A spiritual gift is that what a soul receives supernaturally for this purpose requires the action of given love, for GOD is love. (Giving of Love unto each other) to be *replenished* of *love* by the gift from above His/his glowing flowing. Spiritual energy is a very important aspect of anyone's soul in life. Allow yourself to use it to your benefit (receive from Him/him). Follow your spiritual path and allow the course change over time. Nothing is written in stone and you need to focus on changing only what must be changed to improve your life. As you experience spiritual growth, (Progressive Energy) you will see that everything does happen for a reason and it only serves to make you stronger in oneness of spirit.

As your energy frequency is below, the energy frequency you attract from above. The further amount of energy you bring to yourself, the level of energy you can gain from the cosmic forces to do spiritual work with. The more energy you have within you, the more energy you can match from above. The longer you let the lack of energy build up, the longer it will take to build up energy so build this energy from within Him/him in tradition. Rejoice, enjoy life allow the spirit to lead you.

The consciousness of oneself as a spiritual being grows within heart and mind in progressive stages of self-revelation. At one stage, it may be related to knowledge of oneself as having a relationship with the spiritual world, with GOD, or with the divine presence within the world in which we live. At another, it may be experienced as an awareness of ourselves as souls and of others as souls, joined in a sacred dance of life. Yet both kinds of awareness can become more detailed and more embodied. They can become an expression of our own, intimate clairvoyance which allows us to see and to know the energetic effect of whatever we do.

Rejoice in Chief Unifeatherrock "he that is chief, as he that doth serve His/his living water" he that leads in the relationship with the spiritual world, in a dance of life, full of spiritual fruit of his loins and virile energy. Chief Unifeatherrock communicates a message of wisdom, moved by spirit known their energy from within him. Our soul's are in and of GOD, in Oneness of His Spirit of love.

We are to realize the need to love, **haply flee after him**, dance the dance of life with energy on appointed days lead to do so of Chief Unifeatherrock in tradition. It's always refreshing to have within you the best of what GOD has made within him, His/his (fruit of the Spirit) (Fruit of his loins). The best things in life are free; enjoy of them coming from within Him/him in thy life of love and love of life.

I am free: what spirit is within that is what you feel and what you are. His truth has set your soul free; worship Him in spirit and in truth. Let go of all that is not His truth, his fruit of loins is His free gift that keeps on giving from his everlasting to her everlasting love and life. ***We give our thankfulness to you Lord in advance***. To enjoy our life's in tradition of good habits on appointed days in the sacred dance of life with your Love added into our souls. (You feel me in you, I feel you in me of oneness) For this love is now flowing within us as soul mates.

Prov. 3: 18 She is a tree of life to the man that lay hold upon her: and happy is every man that retaineth her.

Follow your spiritual path *healingtree*, *flee after him haply*, speak to your rock, twice a week and he will emanate into you that is made by GOD from within him Chief Unifeatherrock that is a gift given at the monument of want and need. We as soul mates are free, to follow this Spirit. Draw up His/his salvation from within him drinketh of these glowing flowing living waters of love and life with *delight* from GOD the creator. This virile energy is me and I am this together, our souls exist in oneness you feel me for I am this and this is me, now this spirit within is refreshing new love and life and life of love is now within you.

HEALINGTREE

She is as a tree of life, precious to the man (soul mate) that holds her. In oneness: a gift from GOD. She as a healingtree prospers, when she is nurtured by living water. This spirit that is within her is like *SAP* in the healingtree, and thus replenished.
Significances of TWO Equaling "ONENESS"

A spiritual gift is anything that a person (soul) can do supernaturally well.

Deuteronomy 12:6 There in the presence of the LORD your **GOD**, you and your families shall eat ,drink and shall rejoice in everything you have put your hand to, because the LORD your **GOD** has blessed you.

Gifts of healing: Supernatural ability to bring or release healing to a person in their mind body and soul. Lord JESUS, the mediator of this covenant; enjoyed by all in JESUS.

Proverbs: 3

15 She is more precious than rubies: and all the things thou canst desire are not to be compared unto her.
16 Length of days is in her right hand; and in her left hand riches and honour.
17 Her ways are ways of pleasantness, and all her paths are peace.
18 She is a tree of life to them that lay hold upon her: and happy is every man that retaineth her.

Healing, assessed spiritually, emotionally, mentally or otherwise, is a process which involves more than just the action of cells.

According to the Bible, Abraham, the father of Judaism, Islam and Christianity, *healed a man named Abimelech, by his wives and his maidservants through* **drinking natural medicines and prayer.** The words heal, healed, and healing occurs 132 times in the King James Version of the Holy Bible. There are also non-believers who hold that healing is the result of more than just the action of cells on their own, and may be the result of thought, spiritual agency, etc.

The term "faith healing" is sometimes used in reference to the belief of some Christians who hold that GOD heals people through the power of the Holy Spirit, often involving the *"laying on of hands"*. In the four gospels in the Christian Bible, JESUS is said to cure physical ailments well outside the capacity of first century medicine, most explicitly in the case of "a woman who had had a discharge of blood for twelve years, and who had suffered much under many physicians, and had spent all that she had, and was not better but rather grew worse. JESUS endorsed the use of the medical assistance of the time (*drinking of natural medicines*) when he praised the fictitious Good Samaritan for acting as a physician, telling his disciples to go and do the same thing that the Samaritan did in the story. The healing in the gospels is referred to as a sign to prove his divinity and to foster belief in Himself as the Christ.

However, when asked for other types of miracles, JESUS refused some but granted others, in consideration of the motive of the request, but He healed all present every single time, sometimes determining whether they had faith that he would heal them, but the sole contributing factor was His faith for them. JESUS commanded his followers to heal the sick, and said that signs such as healing were evidence of faith.   M a r k 16:17-18; Matthew 10:8.

In its healing form, *the laying on of hands* is based on biblical precedent set by JESUS. JESUS would walk for days, offering his healing power to peasants and whores, alike. Both Christian and non- Christian faith healers will lay hands on people when praying for healing, and often the name of JESUS is invoked as the spiritual agency through which the healing of physical ailments is believed to be obtained.   Ref. Wikipedia

Tree of life (Healing Tree) is an individual soul, usually distinguished by, her position which is as a treasure of wishes, offerings and pleasantness. Such a Healing Tree is identified as possessing a special natural spiritual value.

Wishes or healings are accessed by sending energy through channels of the mind, body and soul. These channels are dormant in most; she that does manifest her gifts have active or open channels. This "vortex of energy" can use the natural or spiritual power within herself will be replenished by her soul mate can replenish her spiritual energy power from within his living water energy that throbs.

Due to limitation, she that over-uses her gift quickly collapses when she over spends her own natural energy. She is replenished of power from within her soul mate when she receives. This gift in measure received individually is of Him/him by those who seek Him and is given in relation to each owns worthiness therefore all is relative. (Significances of TWO)

Healing Tree using her healing vortex of energy is emanating a flow to encourage a mind, body and soul to do quickly what it would naturally do. For the recipient (soul), this results in the near- instantaneous healing of minor injuries or illness. Major injuries or illness, may take many healing flowing treatments.

This healing gift of energy can repair damages due to injury or illness, of the mind, body and souls but cannot replace a missing limb or reverse birth defects. Healing energy only speeds natural recovery.

Scarring may be reduced by the use of healing but not eliminated.

Natural or supernatural medicines are any substance used as a remedy in treating disease, preventive, curing and improving with preserving health. There are natural spirit enhancers coming from nature when used wisely and correctly can increase your chances of finding your true destinies. Therefore everything or a gift that GOD has created is good, full of his blessing and spirit within and has a definite purpose. (Matt.7:7) JESUS said: Ask, and it shall be given you; seek, and ye shall find; knock, and it shall be opened unto you. Open your mind body and soul of giving/receive of **GOD**s love His/his gift for you to be given into you to refill (replenish) you of this spirit twice a week.

Mind's eye

The phrase "mind's eye" refers to the human ability for visual perception, imagination, visualization, and memory, or, in other words, one's ability to "see" things with the mind. One can say (Out of sight out of mind; insight in mind.)

Physical basis

The biological foundation of the mind's eye is not fully understood. fMRI studies have shown that the lateral geniculation nucleus and the V1 area of the visual cortex are activated during mental imagery tasks. The visual pathway is not a one-way street. Higher areas of the brain can also send visual input back to neurons in lower areas of the visual cortex... As humans, we have the ability to see with the mind's eye -to have a perceptual experience in the absence of visual input. For example, PET scans have shown that when subjects, seated in a room, imagine they are at their front door starting to walk either to the left or right, activation begins in the visual association cortex, the parietal cortex, and the prefrontal cortex - all higher cognitive processing centers of the brain.

Not all humans have this ability. With eyes closed, some humans report that they can visualize, or imagine, detailed scenery that is not just a memory. Others however, cannot. These humans report that while details of visual memories can be recalled (with eyes open), the images themselves cannot be brought up, even with eyes closed.

Philosophy

The use of the phrase mind's eye does not imply that there is a single or unitary place in the mind or brain where visual consciousness occurs. Various philosophers have criticized this view others, have proposed that the brain's electromagnetic field is consciousness itself, thus causing the perception of a unitary location.

(Ref) wikipedia

SEE IN SPIRITUAL JOURNEY

We have gotten so far away from our natural origin of spirituality therefore we must go back in order to correctly advance.

Seek and you will find, believe and you will receive spiritual journey. We know you're out there, you know we are here all of your spirits are so pretty, all of your spirits are so happy. Spirits take us with you; out of sight out of mind yet insight in mind is truly where we want them to be consciously and sub consciously. The good spirits are just here never ending, never forceful and always helpful to those who seek them and know how to find them. One may be under a mild state of hypnosis sub consciously and still be conscious even though being controlled by the sub conscious mind. The spirit can be found in the sub conscious mind that contains nothing of the conscious mind. The only thing moving in the moment is the Spiritual Journey. Find the **GOD** given spirit within by telling JESUS you totally trust Him with your soul and all of the good is in the flesh. Therefore the spiritual journey is inside of you without distance, all are in one of spiritual journey. The spirit is free floating moving forward as free spirit within. One can have visual perception, visualization, and memory, the ability to "*see*" things with the mind within the glorious journey. For of this **GOD** given gift in measure you are a treasure to **GOD** in his spirit of his purpose. Spirits love it when they finally get our attention because that is their purpose to serve us in journey. Keep beauty in mind and your vision will always be kind. Focus in tradition and stay focused.

SUMMARY: To summarize is to perceive understanding.

GRATTITUDE: To show appreciation

We thank GOD for you and for you being shown to us. The perception of a Spiritual Journey comes through as the body actually going somewhere because of seeing so much beauty along the way yet the flesh travels nowhere. The mind takes the journey as the body is at total rest/peace. Therefore the body is connected to the *mind's eye* only in spirit. Going nowhere fast is actually in essence going somewhere with the glowing flow of delight and energy of the delight.

Spiritual Journeys are mainly for the soul to become replenished so afterwards it can help the mind to therefore help the flesh.

Proof That GOD Does Exist (Albert Einstein)

Romans 13: 1 - 2 (Higher Powers)

Albert Einstein was a very beautiful soul and a true genius who showed *no vanity*. He gave us so much by staying connected to the origin of all souls where The Kingdom of **GOD exists in the Light of Holy Spirit.** Answers came freely to him as he would freely seek them in The Light of The Holy Spirit. **He'd sit for hours just seeking and connecting unto The Higher Powers.** He knew that all souls have a cover of flesh and blood. Some souls are recognized as being lost which is the absence of glow from the light. As Einstein we are to sincerely Trust JESUS totally, humbly forgive all, accept and tolerate all and stay connected to *keep the glow in our souls.* The saving of the soul =Salvation. (See illustration of white glowing cross in "Focus"). Amen

Einstein had so much integrity and determination through good and bad times in his lifetime here on earth. *Earth is our second origin of reality. The Kingdom of GOD is our first origin as the soul comes first; flesh comes second.* Romans 8 & Matthew 6:33 Seek ye first the Kingdom of **GOD.**

Misunderstanding, Lacking Romans 8

We must be born of water and spirit. Because we are all born from water in the womb *first* we have come to misunderstand where Spirit is to come first, being true purpose for our existence, not flesh. The flesh gives the soul a cover; an image and a chance to serve GOD.

(1 Thes. 5:23) Holy (Wholly) Spirit=Whole; Complete, Divine Light, Trust, Forgiveness, Compassion, Mercy and Understanding, Focused on Righteousness

Opposite

Unholy, the absence of light, incomplete, darkness, disobedience, deception and illusive, lies and hatred, the absence of The Holy Spirit.

Einstein ran out of time but time goes on so we are here to pick up where he left off. Yes, Amen, we most definitely do know that we have been freely given a revelation to freely give to all who seek Spiritual Answers. This is an act of kindness upon spreading The Gospel=The Spell of The Higher Powers who exist in The Kingdom of **GOD.** Romans 13, 1& 2 The ABSOLUTE TRUTH OF THE ORIGIN of all souls is here for we are created in **GODs IMAGE**.

Einstein may know that we were given this Glory of **GOD that we are to freely give by posting it on our web site. He may have been among the saints and angels who accompanied The White Glowing Cross of Changes that came to us so freely on Saturday, October 02, 1993.**

**** (The Original Footage of The Revelation Freely Given is on record)

Relative: Prov.18:4 Therefore **GOD** knows his spirit of love grows when his living water flows. That is why we are called ONE of the same. The body is one of flowing spirit in the flesh, with different purpose, all made from star (light of past) dust. For what is flesh without spirit of life within? From dust we came to dust we return. We do not live without flowing living water added into the dust. Einstein ref. "$E=MC^2$"*argument of* *theory*: **Energy** is flowing spirit, **Mass** is flesh and **GOD; A SOUL,** is the light. (Relativity **E=MG**)

****The word, Soul comes from Solar from the Sun from The LIGHT.

GOD given *soul mate* of *love* for men

John 4:24: **GOD** *is* a Spirit: and they that worship *Him* must worship *Him* in spirit and in truth.

1Corin.11:3 It is written in the *Bible*, that humans are required to follow as tradition, that a wife be obedient to her husband, and in return of this, he should love her body as his own. (oneness) (wife: she is flesh of my flesh and spirit)

Soul: An entity, spiritual part of a person.

Mate: A matched pair, couple or union, to share the joys of life with appreciation of one to the other. For man & woman do not live by bread alone.

Glowing: A still burning or with life.

Flowing: To transfer from one's own possession to that of another. The giving/receiving as a gift is a great honor. (there is none greater than the creator)

Glowing flowing spirit of *love* within her mate is food for her soul and flesh. This is filled with **GODs** *love* in the flesh a spirit of *love* within the flowing glowing of **GODs** making. This spirit that is within is like *SAP in the Tree of life (healing tree)*, filled with spiritual goodness, power and spirit within. His/his mate is thus *replenished*, and *rerewarded*. This contains power that is with healing, that is made by **GOD**, filled with a measure of what his mate needs. This glowing flowing spirit of *love* is given for his mate to enjoy freely and abundantly, of this will be a blessing and *rerewarding* of both its bliss. For of men this is their **GOD** given purpose to share freely and enjoy this glowing in good habits. With purpose of enjoying the glowing feeling of the glorious power of the flowing into his mate, as it is **GODs** purpose as a glorious blessing to his mate to receive from her mate, for this action each are blessed by feeling the glowing spirit of *love* of life in the flesh. Cherishes every glowing and realize that this is now a wonderment growing inside each, as a chance in life to assist **GOD** in a miracle of His/his making. Seek in view of **GOD** living joyful *love*, holy and pleasing to Him this glorious spiritual act of worship with devotion in good habits. Walk in His spirit of purpose, knowing it is of *anointing* from Him, do not let this **GOD** given blessing become polluted. Soul mates receive this as a blessing of **GODs** spirit of *love* within soul mates. Therefore everything He has created is good, full of His blessings having a definite purpose of spirit within, the spirit of *love* within glowing flowing raises us up to what we can be; utmost best friends & lovers of the gift of life and love unto each other.

GOD given *soul mate* of *love* for woman

I his mate am aware of glowing flowing spirit of *love* am free and ready to receive from my mate what He/he prepared for me. Be still and trust **JESUS**, for within the stillness of His Spirit His/his *Love* always can be found.

Our *love* takes us higher I (his mate) am free with spark of good habits, for our *love* to become higher from the glowing fire. Mates need to *let go*, we go higher in spiritual glowing fire. The spirits want to be with us, just *let it go* into the spirit of glowing. For this glowing flowing spirit of *love* will add into our glowing. Mates do this in good habits in *love* of glowing spiritual life in us both is bliss. To receive a moment that **GOD** has created and given to us is a blessing for only **GOD** can take them away.

For glowing spirit in me lets my mate know the spirit of *love* is with power to let go and enjoy the *love* of life that I have within me is ready to enjoy glowing and sharing therefore no polluting is now within me. When his beginning is finished or the end of his flowing will come to start a new beginning of glowing of me (his mate). Insight in mind is truly where I want to be in good habits. **GOD** given spirit of powers that throb, I receive lets him, my soul mate know what I wanted and what I needed, to be replenished by his *love* now within me. To have a glowing flowing voyage within me is its purpose. Through our receiving we are complete. For of this action mates become as one body of this glowing flowing spirit. We submit to **GOD** and the soul mate submits to one another of our free will.

The glowing spirit is a free floating free spirit with glowing *love*. The gathering of **GOD**s spirit within moves us forward of free glowing spirit of *love* within. It's a living substance, it's a given substance and it's not to be wasted, all the goodness is not a secret, **GOD** made the glowing flowing spirit of *love* for us. For we don't want to be heartbreaker's to **GOD** but *love* maker's of **GOD,** raises us up to what we can be. For it is necessary to us for us and of us to give of ourselves unto one another in spirit and flesh to satisfy tradition. Therefore no waste or stagnant *love* exists. The flow of the spirit must go on as with the flesh. Therefore **GOD**s spirit of *love* is inside the soul mates is one spirit. This is me and I am this together, we both exist you can feel me for I am in this and of this His /his flowing now within me.

Fruit of the Spirit

Galatians 5:18

The fruit of the Spirit is; *love, joy, peace, patience, kindness, goodness, faithfulness, gentleness and self-control.* Against such things there is no law.

These Gifts are understood to be manifestations given at the time of need for the purpose at hand. Each individual if open and willing to be used by the Spirit will eventually be used at the discretion of the Spirit.

Romans 12: They are meted out to all for Service in the Body and considered Operational in their application.

1 Cor. 12:6- It has also been said that these particular Gifts have not been restricted to the Body of Christ but have been given to all souls ever born. "And there are diversities of operations, but it is the same GOD which worketh all in all." The word "all" being the same as the "all" in "All have sinned and come short of the Glory of GOD" and JESUS died for "all".

"A spiritual gift is anything that a person (soul/spirit) can do supernaturally well."

First find the GOD given fruit of the spirit within your flesh therefore all of the good shall be in the flesh according to his purpose. We human's (Souls) are in the kingdom of GOD filled with his spirit, with different callings of his purpose to His will. Humans are of free fruit of the spirit to do his called purpose, of them that love His spirit within.

Saint Augustine summarized this when he wrote "Love God, and do as thou wilt".

1 Cor. 13:4-7 Paul the Apostle glorified love as the most important virtue of all. Describing love in the famous poem in 1 Corinthians he wrote, "Love is patient, love is kind. It does not envy, it does not boast, it is not proud. It is not rude, it is not self-seeking, it is not easily angered, it keeps no record of

wrongs. Love does not delight in evil but rejoices with the truth. It always protects, always trusts, always hopes, and always perseveres."

Luke 17:21 Neither shall they say, Lo here! or, lo there! for, behold, the kingdom of God is within you.
Galatians 5:18 But if ye be led of the Spirit, ye are not under the law.

Mark 12: 28-31
29 And JESUS answered him, The first of all the commandments is, Hear, O Israel; The Lord our God is one Lord:
30 And thou shalt love the Lord thy God with all thy heart, and with all thy soul, and with all thy mind, and with all thy strength: this is the first commandment.
31 And the second is like, namely this, Thou shalt love thy neighbour as thyself. There is none other commandment greater than these.

Job 32:18-19
18 For I am full of matter, the spirit within me constraineth me.
19 Behold, my belly is as wine which hath no vent; it is ready to burst like new bottles. (The need to let go with flowing from within)

Song of Solomon 5:2
I sleep, but my heart waketh: it is the voice of my beloved that knocketh, saying, Open to me, my sister, my love, my dove, my undefiled: for my (god) head is filled with dew, and my locks with the drops of the night.
Bible employs the term "dew" in this sense in such verses as declaring, for example, that the people should follow only a king who was virile enough to be full of the "*dew*" of youth. (semen /creator of youth)

Psalm 110:3 Thy people shall be willing in the day of thy power, in the beauties of holiness from the womb of the morning: thou hast the *dew* of thy youth.

Dew was once thought to be a sort of rain that fertilized the earth and, in time, became a metaphor for of men. *The wife feeds her husband who returns to her his dew, the milk of human kindness.* She keeps him healthy he keeps her healthy in body and spirit of love within in oneness. (his returning of Fathers making for her)

Proverbs: 3 13-22
13 ¶ Happy *is* the man *that* findeth wisdom, and the man *that* getteth understanding.
14 For the merchandise of it *is* better than the merchandise of silver, and the gain thereof than fine gold.
15 *She is* more precious than rubies: and all the things thou canst desire are not to be compared unto her.
16 Length of days *is* in her right hand; *and* in her left hand riches and honour.
17 Her ways *are* ways of pleasantness, and all her paths *are* peace.
18 *She is* a tree of life to them that lay hold upon her: and happy is every man that retaineth her. (Healing Tree)
19 The LORD by wisdom hath founded the earth; by understanding hath he established the heavens.
20 By his knowledge the depths are broken up, for clouds drop down dew.
21 ¶ My son, let not them depart from thine eyes: keep sound wisdom and discretion:
22 So shall they be life unto thy soul, and grace to thy neck.

John 4:14 But whosoever drinketh of the water that I shall give shall never thirst; but the water that I shall give shall be of a well of water springing up into everlasting life.

GOD LOVES

GOD Loves: With His Love He created all therefore All is His and He is All.

GOD makes His presence known in all senses and also in every sunrise and sunset.

Smell: In the forest at dusk or dawn within the dew droplets, fragrances of the pine trees for example or honey suckle vines perfume the air. The breathing in of the sensational fragrances enhances all other senses and lifts the spirit of the soul.

Colors: The magnificent beauty of the colors of light is reflected in every rainbow, prism, sunrise and sunset. The colors of light are what creates the color of the flowers' blossom along with the liquid of course which is the reflector. The sun's rays have healing powers. For example the impurities are removed from the water being absorbed by the suns' rays from lakes, rivers, streams and etc. This is natures' filtering process to eventually store the moisture as clouds to bring clean (rain) living water to the earth.

Texture: The softness of the touching of delicate precious baby skin and the softness of the breasts that feed the baby mother's milk. The texture of a baby chicks' feather is also very soothing to touch.

Music: For example: Beethoven's Fifth Symphony in man's music so touches the soul. The birds sing sweetly in the trees, tree frogs and bugs in the trees joining in harmony to create a heartfelt rhythm of one unique sound such as nature's orchestra.

Taste: Biting into a ripe juicy piece of succulent fruit, drinking a refreshing beverage when extremely thirsty or tasting for the very first time as a baby nursing mother's milk or tasting a sweet lollipop to bring joy as the baby also brings joy to others.

So many clues are there for us in nature for **GOD** wants us to pay attention to and observe.

Five elements: Earth, Fire, Water, Air and *Love*. Love comes from the sun as it warms our bodies even at night when it can't be seen as two bodies embrace *connecting their energies* of the spirit to heal the soul to heal the body.

****Anything that touches the soul also warms the heart and vs. versa. John 4:8: He that loveth not knoweth not **GOD**; for **GOD** is *love*.

Significance of Two

Significances of TWO Equaling "ONE"

Two ultimate processes make up our Universe. Star Dust (with living water within) and Energies (with Spirit of Light).

To make up Planet Earth there are two processes being Father GOD and Mother Nature to equal "ONE" very complete; whole planet.

The sun that heats the air draws up water from the earth that contains the elements that are used in making living water, *filtering and adding into* that makes the rain must be done in two processes.

Therefore keeps the living water *flowing* (rain) fresh on the earth. This process of flowing prevents polluting, spoil or stagnant living water. This living water is for us to drink, replenishment and to nourish us and water gardens everywhere.

Within humans the same is true the flow of living water must continue in spirit and flesh, therefore no pollution, spoil or stagnant living water exist. The flow of the spirit within must go on with the flesh. All that GOD the creator makes is good and from GOD, the nutrients are of His making to nourish and grow in Him and of Him.

It takes TWO

Example: (1+1=2) (one to give, one to receive) (one to give love, one to receive love) (one to teach, one to be taught) (one to be partaken of, one to be replenished by) (one to make, one to use) (one to seek, one to find) (male, female) (one to look, one to be looked at) (spirit within, living water) etc. etc.

No matter how you *shape it*, or where *it comes from*, or what *contains it*, or what is *contained within it*, or what of its *purpose of flowing*, it's still living water. Everything **GOD** has created is good and all relative by spirit of life within water for without *spirit within* the living water (semen /creator) there will be no life.

When you think of the words for example: "Can't see the forest for the trees."

This simply means that you are looking at something but not truly seeing what you are looking at. The Key to *seeing* and not just looking is to have the *Spirit within your* seeing the something you are looking at. It will be seen in a state of absolute reality instead of a mere illusion of reality.

The sub conscious mind must be the leader of the mind's thinking in order to see clearly. This process is including the mind's eye and the instincts that are found in all sub consciousness. For Example: "There's more there than what meets the eye."

Focusing on Righteousness To do it right we must *focus*.

How do we focus? To focus is to *become aware of* and *concentrate, totally*. Let go of all other thoughts that interfere with the process of focusing. No distractions whatsoever can interfere with totally focusing.

We must look at the overall picture as "ONE." We look at it as a *whole*, not in pieces/parts. Really look at it good. If something is broken it needs repairs because it won't work.

Our minds are similar. They may work but not properly. They need repairs. Every day our minds need fixing. Why? So we will do what we do right.

GOD's Time is our time to equal Sacrifice. We spend time with Him making His Time, ours. We are both sacrificing to do so. (Oneness)

With GOD's Time leading we can let go of all of the insignificant stuff we keep holding on to taking up space and time and cluttering up our minds. It's so easy to allow our emotions to run wild when not making love. Keep emotions at a low level when humbling oneself unto The Fathers Holy Spirit.

Trust and Obey

1 Thes.5:22-24 Our instincts stay sharp by seeking and finding *Thy Wholly Spirit*. Once found, Trusting is the Key. We must completely trust in Thy Wholly Spirit that dwells within. The Soul is asleep without being found and awakened by Thy Wholly Spirit. Be still, wait patiently and trust Him and He shall come out of the stillness of the light to find you.

Free Will

When we choose to become aware we have chosen to recognize in a sense all we have become aware of.

Full Circle

Awareness, acceptance, tolerance, patience and The Love of GOD shall bring understanding as to why we are to forgive all as all in turn shall forgive all.

Could this be so that choosing not to forgive becomes a grudge being held that also becomes a curse? Absolutely! We not only curse another but ourselves as well. Wishing something bad to happen to another is in essence also wishing something bad to happen to you. Life is a boomerang effect in general. What goes out comes back around eventually to either bite you or bless you. Do all with The Love of Him and many blessings shall come out of what is therefore being done. AMEN

John 14: 9 **JESUS said,** "If you have seen Me you have also seen My Father." (The substance of the Father is restored to the Son.) John 5:17- Hitherto: change in which individuals of a species mature past adulthood and take on unseen traits. [**GOD**s gift to men (semen/creator of life) within]

The following saying is God-given by the Wholly Spirit to proclaim that we take up our cross (our soul) to follow JESUS which is connecting our soul unto His (the cross) by handing it all over to Him in order to be saved.
HIS ALL WILL NOT BE LOST WHEN ALL WILL REMEMBER HIS CROSS

GOD had a definite purpose for His crucifixion on the cross in The name of JESUS Christ. This is the greatest purpose of all as He forgave all of our sins at the cross; in turn all (we) are to forgive all of their sins as well. The greatest commandment is to love **GOD** with all our hearts and all that we are.

An old saying: "One can lead a horse to water but can't make it drink" (of its own free will at that moment). One can say that the horse is not aware of the water and its purpose to drink. One can say the horse will drink when it thirsts. One can say in faith the horse will drink in free will. One can say of free will I lead the horse to the water, in free will for the horse to drink. It's all part of **GOD**s purpose for the horse to drink water in free will in any given moment. One can say in faith I reject the word can't.

Good thing and bad thing pending on who is making the choice and whether or not one is seeking and trusting **JESUS** in all they are and shall become every moment. If one can seek and find a little spark of Joy each day in some simple way then the love of **GOD** will surely come their way Matt. 6:33. Knowing His Presence and experiencing His Peace allows one to make decisions in life that conform to His Will. When one chooses to practice seeking the Presence of Him, one will have access to information bringing answers. The information is available to all who seek Him where purpose can be found as **GODs Will** to control our actions as human with souls.

Man is of **GOD**s creation as are all other living things of this earth. He is spirit and love, man is made in His image (spirit and love). **GOD** is *free will* therefore also man is (*free will*) all other of nature are of His *free will* and purpose. He/he is thy creator/semen of all in all is His/his creation we are of His/his. (The gift of life)

Words

Without the words there can be no letter. For our words are given by spirit. What do these words say to you? Words are not what they say without spirit of your understanding of the spirit in the words. The spirit has only your understanding of the words given by the spirit.

John 4:24: **GOD** *is* a Spirit: and they that worship *Him* must worship *Him* in spirit and in truth. John 4:8: He that loveth not knoweth not **GOD**; for **GOD** is *love*.

Utterance: The power or style of speaking, or written language. (word) Symbols: Something that stands for or represents another thing.

Alphabet: The letters of a language, arranged in a traditional order. A system of: characters, signs, or symbols used in letters. The first elements used as a branch of knowledge. "The Fruit of knowledge"

If a word is misspelled in the dictionary, how would we ever know? If Webster wrote the first dictionary, where did he find the words?

That our way of being human and the way the world is for us are given by the assumptions that come along with our language.

Gen 1: In the beginning was the word and the word was the spirit of **GOD** and said it was **good** for food. And the word become flesh and JESUS said John 6:56: He that eateth my flesh, and drinketh my blood, dwelleth in me, and I in him.

The difference from man and animal is their understanding. Animals can and do communicate one to another in some way according to their kind with meaning of their understanding, meaning of their nature or instinct, shown to them by their kind of natural selection from generations past. The smartest and strongest that adjusted and learn how to live in the world that **GOD** had made for them, birds in the air, fish in the sea and others of the land survive.

GOD gave unto man dominion over all of His making. Man is of His creation as are all other living things of this earth. He is spirit and love, man is made in His image (spirit and love). He is free will therefore also man, all other of nature are of His free will and purpose. **GOD** gave unto man utterance the spirit of symbols to pass down or to teach others not yet passed. Therefore this became the word, the beginning of teaching the spirit and love of Him. The ***Bible*** (His Story) holds in remembrance the spirit that is given to us the most loved book of our kind. This is the beginning of teaching of His spirit to mankind. Therefore this book in words is the spirit and love of Him from within Him. (thy gift of His/his love and life)

The Gospel According to You

There's a sweet old story translated for men, but written in the long, long ago:

The Gospel according to Matthew, Mark, Luke and John of Christ and His mission!

You are writing a Gospel, a chapter each day, by deeds that you do, by words that you say. Men read what you write, whether faithless or true. Say what is the Gospel according to you.

Men read and admire the Gospel of Christ, with its love so unfailing and true, but what do they say and what do they think of the Gospel according to you?

This is a wonderful story that Gospel of love, as it shines in the Christ-life divine and O that it's true might be told again in the story of your life and mine.

Unselfishness mirrors in every scene, love blossoms on every sod and back from its vision the heart comes to tell the wonderful goodness of GOD.

You are writing each day a letter to men: spirit in words in oneness

Take care that the writing is true. This is the only Gospel some men will read, the Gospel according to you. AMEN

Ruled by influence by the vast majority, brainwashing has us in a box, whether we are aware of it or not. Instead we should be thinking outside the box going with the flowing of glowing spirit from within.

At home we are the minority not infected by the majority (the child in us) before the clinches of society's strong influence told us to get in the box. The majority of the influence makes up the karma given off by the spirits around. They get inside the unprotected soul.

Granted before our receiving of Him we were not aware of all of the beautiful spirit flowing out there all around us. They love it when they finally get our attention because that is part of their purpose to serve us.

I am that I am

GOD has given unto to me all what I am today in this moment as I am and all I will ever be in this moment is from Him, I will not be what I was yesterday, nor will I be the same as I am in this moment, for tomorrow is of moments not yet passed. For when I receive the moment or the measure of the moment that He has *given,* or *gives now* or *ever will give* is in his purpose of and for the moment. The *moment does not move as all passes through it in stillness of the moment* as time stands still.

Time:

A dimension that man created is time however the only way time can be viewed in mans' creation *is by using a manmade object.* In theory not yet proven a minute is sixty seconds, an hour is 60 minutes and a day is 24 hours. We are in the year 2010 (approx.) according to mans' theory.

To GOD, time is something He has been *aware* of from the beginning, the time in between and the end of time. He *is eternal and exists outside of time.* (1 year=1 complete trip around our sun)

Rev.1: I am Alpha and Omega, the beginning and the ending, saith the Lord, Which is, which was, and which is to come, the Almighty.

John 4:24 GOD is *Holy Spirit* and they that worship Him must worship Him in spirit and in truth.

Spirit Collectors: We have become *spirit collectors.* Beautiful spirits can be found all around us all every moment in trusting JESUS. Only good can come from trusting Him. We have been graciously given a very special gift while finding the glory of GOD. As us gathering His spirit within, it moves us forward at a *variable* speed of flow within flowing, we must be still in this moment, seeking His giving in spirit of His flowing.

Granted before our receiving of Him we were not *aware* of all of the beautiful spirit flowing out there all around us. The Spirits love it when they finally get our attention because that is their purpose to serve us.

Note: The measure received individually of Him by those who seek Him is given in relation to worthiness therefore all is relative.

We are to thank GOD for all the blessing that is of His making. We are commented in strong spirit to do His called purpose in the flesh. We walk in His spirit of His purpose, we believe His purpose is of anointing that He/he gives to us and not have this **GOD** given blessing or bliss become polluted. We are in His spirit when we receive this as a blessing to us, of His spirit within us. (Oneness)

Daniel 12: Another concept worth reconsidering is that "knowing" will lead to wisdom. This drives us to get to the bottom of the truth. But maybe it's better not to understand everything. Maybe the point of life is not about getting to the bottom of it. Maybe it's simply about living for the sake of living. Maybe life doesn't have any deeper meaning than the meaning that you give it each moment. It can be liberating to keep the mystery intact instead of wanting to unravel it, explain it, write it down and proclaim you've uncovered the ultimate "truth". For me, in any case, saying "I don't know," sitting in silence and being open to listen offers more insight than any analysis or a logical explanation. It is best to keep a clear head that has been cleansed therefore being *filtered* through meditation. This is necessary in order to obtain the measure of knowledge that becomes you to therefore be-come your moment in giving/ receiving of glowing flowing spirit of love and life.

He/he is the dew of the earth. Dew (semen) doesn't exist for its own pleasure. It must be flowing within someone other than himself the creator; only then does it fulfill its purpose. The transfer from one to another giving/receiving of this gift is a Great honor. (Within sharing love from within thy self)

(There is none greater than LOVE)

(Hallelujah) Praise GOD from whom all blessing flow. (His/ his flowing)

Flowing: To transfer from one's own possession to that of another. The giving/ receiving from within is an honor. (There is none greater flowing)

Utterance

The power or style of speaking, or written language. (the word)

Glory Psalm 24:5-10

5 He shall receive the blessing from the LORD, and righteousness from the GOD of his *salvation*.
6 This is the generation of them that seek him that seek thy face, O Jacob.
7 ¶ Lift up your heads, O ye gates; and be ye lift up, ye *everlasting* doors; and the King of glory shall come in.
8 Who is this King of glory? The LORD strong and mighty, the LORD mighty in battle.
9 Lift up your heads, O ye gates; even lift them up, ye *everlasting* doors; and the King of glory shall come in.
10 Who is this King of glory? The LORD of hosts, he is the King of glory.

John 1:14 The Word became flesh and made his dwelling among us. We have seen his glory, the glory of the One and only, who came from the Father, full of grace and truth. (the fullness of the godhead bodily)

Revelation 21:11 It shone with the glory of him, and its brilliance was like that of a very precious jewel, like a jasper, clear as crystal. (living water/semen)

Revelation 21:23 The city does not need the sun or the moon to shine on it, for the glory of GOD gives it light, and the Lamb is its lamp.

Habakkuk 2:14 For the earth will be filled with the knowledge of the glory of the LORD, as the waters cover the sea. (the glory of living water is semen/creator)

Psalm 84:11 For the LORD GOD is a sun and shield; the LORD bestows favor and honor; no good thing does he withhold from those whose walk is blameless.

2 Corinthians 3:18 And we, who with unveiled faces all reflect the Lord's glory, are being transformed into his likeness with ever-increasing glory, which comes from the Lord, who is the Spirit. (His/his living water/creator)

The root word in Hebrew is kabod, meaning "weight" or "heaviness." The same word is then used to express GOD's majesty and honour, or GOD's miraculous power that throbs. GOD's glory is often associated with displays of light, e.g. thunderbolts, fire, brightness and glowing.

Divine glory is an important motif throughout Judeo-Christian theology, where GOD is regarded as the most glorious being. Since they are created in the Image of GOD, human beings can share or participate in divine glory as image-bearers. Like a mirror, the human person reflects GOD's glory, though imperfectly. (Thus Christians are instructed to "let your light shine before men, that they may see your good works, and glorify your Father/creator who is in heaven.")

Glory (religion), in Judeo-Christian religious tradition, the manifestation of GOD's presence; see also Hod (Kabbalah)

Glory: A term in Christian art for a halo surrounding the whole body of a person.

Glory Be to the Father (creator), also known as Gloria Patri, a Christian prayer, a doxology or short hymn of praise to GOD in various Christian liturgies

Great honor, praise, or distinction accorded by common consent; renown, something conferring honor or renown.

A highly praiseworthy asset: Your wit is your crowning glory. Adoration, praise, and thanksgiving offered in worship.

Majestic beauty and splendor; resplendence: The sun set in a blaze of glory. The splendor and bliss of heaven: perfect happiness. (Love)

A height of achievement, enjoyment, or prosperity: ancient Rome in its greatest glory.

A halo, nimbus, or aureole is Also called gloriole. intr.v. glo·ried, glo·ry·ing, glo·ries

To rejoice triumphantly; exult: a sports team that gloried in its hard-won victory. (ref) Wikipedia

Grace

In Christianity, grace is "unmerited favor" from GOD. Divine grace is a description of the character of GOD, which is displayed by GOD's gifts to humanity. Grace describes the means by which humans (souls) are granted salvation (and to some, saved from original sin). Grace is of central importance in the theology of Christianity, as well as one of the most contentious issues in Christian sectarianism. The principle of grace is considered as fundamental to Christianity as justice is to Law. The terms "salvation" and "grace" therefore become "virtually synonymous." Yet, grace has never been made part of any Christian except for the Westminster Confession.

This is a consequence of original sin; a sinful nature is inherited; explained as a result of the fall of man through the first sins of Adam and Eve in Eden. Some who reject the story from Genesis as history still agree that humans are born in sin, but the meaning and connotation of this phrase varies widely. *The original state of **grace** enjoyed by the once-good people GOD created has been lost, for them and for their descendants.*

The New Testament word that is usually translated "grace" is in Greek charis (?a???). which literally means "that which affords joy, pleasure, delight, sweetness, (sweet fruit) charm, loveliness". The word was not often used by JESUS himself;

in the canonical Gospels it is attributed to him only in the Gospel of Luke and the Gospel of John. However, the parables attributed to JESUS in the Gospels make clear that JESUS did in fact teach the concept of grace. *More importantly, He told stories that underlined that grace was GOD's to give, GOD's sole prerogative, and that it was freely offered.* (as a gift)(the gift of live)

Psalm 45:2 You are the most excellent of men and your lips have been anointed with grace, since GOD has blessed you forever.

Proverbs 1:9 They will be a garland to grace your head and a chain to adorn your neck. Proverbs 3:22 They will be life for you, an ornament to grace your neck.

Jeremiah 2:13 My people have committed two sins: They have forsaken me, the spring of living water, and have dug their own cisterns, broken cisterns that cannot hold water.

Psalm 36:9 For with you is the fountain of life; in your light we see light.

Praise

Praise is an impassioned exaltation of GOD (ie. a Supreme Being, or Creation), typically as an expression of gratitude for one's life or being. In other cases, praise may be tied to more situational aspects of living, such as health and prosperity.

In Christianity, the word refers specifically to extoling or exalting GOD and his attributes. Praise can be a portion of a service of worship, a period of singing ("praising GOD") usually before the more formal part, hence the term "praise and worship" to describe the whole event.

Praise GOD the Father (Him) from whom all *blessing flow*. (ref) Wikipedia, Suffering

Suffering occurs commonly in the lives of sentient beings, in diverse manners, and often dramatically. As a result, many fields of human activity are concerned, from their own points of view, with some aspects of suffering.

The words pain and suffering are often used both together in different ways. For instance, they may be used as interchangeable synonyms. Or they may be used in 'contradistinction' to one another, as in "pain is inevitable, suffering is optional", or "pain is physical, suffering is mental". Or they may be used to define each other, as in "pain is physical suffering", or "suffering is severe physical or mental pain".

Qualifiers, such as mental, emotional, psychological, and spiritual, are often used for referring to certain types of pain or suffering. In particular, mental pain (or suffering) may be used in relationship with physical pain (or suffering) for distinguishing between two wide categories of pain or suffering. A first caveat concerning such a distinction is that it uses physical pain in a sense that normally includes not only the 'typical sensory experience of physical pain' but also other unpleasant bodily experiences such as itching or nausea. A second caveat is that the terms physical or mental should not be taken too literally: physical pain or suffering, as a matter of fact, happens through conscious minds and involves emotional aspects, while mental pain or suffering happens through physical brains and, being an emotion, involves important physiological aspects.

Words that are roughly synonymic with suffering, in addition to pain, include distress, sorrow, unhappiness, misery, affliction, woe, ill, discomfort, displeasure, disagreeableness, unpleasantness. (The **lack** of His/his grace, glory, bliss and *salvation /orgasm*) or (Long suffering)
(ref) Wikipedia

Righteousness

Righteous, integrity, equity, justice, straightness. The root of tseh'-dek is tsaw-dak', Gesenius's , upright, just, straight, innocent, true, sincere. It is best understood as the product of upright, moral action in accordance with some form of divine plan. person has been "judged" or "reckoned" as leading a life that is pleasing to GOD. Righteousness is also used as an attribute for GOD. (Psalm 2) speaks of one being shielded by GOD and receiving favor because of righteousness.

In the Book of Job the title character is introduced to us as a person who is "perfect" in righteousness. This does not mean that he is sinless."Perfect", in this sense means that his righteousness permeates every relationship of his life as his working principle. After all, righteousness is a matter of relationships - with GOD, with things, and with other people. The biblical definition of righteousness involves the inherent quality of GOD. GOD is right because He is righteous, therefore GOD can only act righteously. In one instance the word means being right; in another it is used to mean doing right; in still another case it means putting right. Job qualifies as a righteous person on each of these counts, so much so that he is commended by GOD as "wholly righteous" or, translated into our terms, "perfect." (ref) Wikipedia, encyclopedia

Flow: To transfer from one's own possession to that of another. The giving/ receiving from within is an honor. (There is none greater)

Happiness / *Blessings* (*Rejoice*): In mystical traditions, especially in advanced spiritual techniques, are related to full balance (conjunction, union, "secret marriage") of inner energy lines (energy channels of a soul or deepest dimension of the human soul).

Isaiah 45:8 (Hallelujah) "You heavens above, rain down righteousness; let the clouds shower it down. Let the earth open wide, let *salvation* spring up, let righteousness grow with it; I, the LORD, have created it. (Living Water / Semen)

For in faith: For it says what it says that I am, for it has what I say that I have, for it will do what it says I can do.

The *fruit of the Spirit* is **love, joy, peace, patience, kindness, goodness, faithfulness, gentleness and self-control.** Against such things there is no law.

John 15:7-8
7 If ye abide in me, and my words abide in you, ye shall ask what ye will, and it shall be done unto you.
8 Herein is my Father glorified, that ye bear much fruit; so shall ye be my disciples.

✟HERAPY PLUS PRAYER

Everlasting Words of JESUS; in RED letters

For in faith and all within is self supported of Scriptures

Semen **A**loe **P**rayer (SAP)

For it is written in words within the books of Testament within Bible "The word of GOD in the world of men" for the understanding or the **Utterance** of the word of GOD. (What do these words say to you?)

Romans 16:25-27

25 Now to him that is of power to stablish you according to my gospel, and the preaching of JESUS Christ, according to the revelation of the mystery, which was kept secret since the world began.
26 But now is made manifest, and by the scriptures of the prophets, according to the commandment of the everlasting GOD, made known to all nations for the obedience of **faith**:
27 To GOD ONLY wise, be the glory through JESUS forever.

Seek His kingdom and His righteousness, and all these things will be given into you. Thy kingdom is within thy kingdom come thy will be done on earth as it is in heaven.

EVERLASTING

Praise GOD from whom all blessing flow. This flowing from *everlasting* is filled with **GODs** love in spirit within His making. This of goodness that is His, forasmuch every drop of His/his making within belongs to Him. As a *gift* from GOD the Father whom all bliss flows *his returning into her for everlasting life*. (Father/creator/semen the gift of life within love)

With this comes truth: the glory of **JESUS** is the fullness of grace and truth. In that He is the truth and the delight within himself *his returning* for her; He is LORD and MASTER. (O LORD bless this living water) as drink indeed.

Semen/creator is living water the substance that dwelleth or circulates through men is his sweet fruit bearing life, is vital to life within men is his hidden wealth of this gift is for her health. She is as a *tree* of life, precious to the man that holds her. In oneness is a gift from GOD the father. She prospers, when she is nurtured by his wealth of his sweet fruit (semen). This spirit within her is like *SAP* and thus she's replenished. (Fathers living water is spiritual replenishment for *soul mates*)

> When JESUS knew in himself that his disciples murmured at it, he said unto them, John 6:61 (Doth this offend you?)

> The substance giving life; creating us
> heals us in flesh and faith.

> *Semen* is the most sacred substance within
> of his returning for her return.

Read to be wise, believe to be right, In Application of faith be wholly and loyal servant unto JESUS. Within His Covenant (Oath of tradition on appointed days)

'Feel Me Heal Me': *What do these words say to you*? Words are not what they say without spirit of your understanding of the spirit in the words. The spirit has only your understanding of the words given by the spirit.

What do you see in your mind's eye when you think of making love (Lust) or a gift from **GOD**, if you think (Lust) you have the box influence in your *mind's eye*. Making love in not what we do, love is where we come from and what we are made of. He does not remove things-He creates them. He created sex in Eden, men and women were made to enjoy each other we are not just body parts but bodies with souls to pleasure each other's body and soul. He wants us to enjoy love and sex but ***not idealize*** it. Love not only pleases us it's what pleases Him for He is love and the spirit within His *soul mates*.

Love is a gift from **GOD** and made within man in oneness from man to emanate this as a *gift* from within him. His flowing semen of love is for her to be *replenished*, and him to be *refreshed,* restored of love by the gift from **GOD** above.

Influenced by a power of manipulative suggestion, brainwashing has put us in a box, whether we are aware of it or not. Instead we should be outside the box going with His flow of the spirit within.

Everything **GOD** has created is good, full of His blessing and spirit within of His love. *He is in you as you are of Him*. Whole and complete is to use the fleshly mind, body and soul to let go and connect to His glowing flow of love. For it is necessary to us for us and of us to give of ourselves unto one another in spirit and flesh to satisfy *tradition*. Therefore no pollution, spoil or stagnant living water (semen) of life of love exists, keep thy gift fresh all within is restored and **rejuvenated**.

GOD did not give us a spirit of *timidity*, but a spirit of power and love. Love is more than a feeling it's a living substance it's a given substance NOT to be polluted / wasted. We give thanks to Him for all in all. Natural and supernatural healing are substances used as a remedy in treating disease, preventive, curing and improving with preserving health. Semen is a natural substance and healing coming from within men made by **GOD** for her, when she enjoys of this substance, she will have increased for her love and destinies from this substance now within her.

Passion: feeling very strongly about a subject or person, usually referring to feelings of intense desire and attraction; be very passionate about something also often applied to a lively eager interest in or admiration for a person, cause, action.

In Christianity, in the New Testament, *lust* it is treated as one of many sins and states of mind. However, it is always distinguished from sexual desire, which in Christianity is a **GOD**-given gift. Lust however, is regarded as a wanton perversion of that gift, and is used to refer to unchecked desire for fornication, adultery, or any sex *outside of marriage or soul mates.*

Saint Augustine stated this when he wrote "Love **GOD**, and do as thou wilt".

Sacred semen: In societies, it's revered because it is believed to be magical. It is also widely believed to be of supernatural origin and is, as a result, considered sacred. Semen is currently and has long been revered by traditions as a very important constituent of human physiology. (ref) (wikipedia)

GODs gift of semen the giver of life and cause of all creation. In other cultures is worshiped as an erect penis. This refers to the life giving semen coming (flowing) out from within the top of the erect Sacred Mount (godhead bodily/penis).

Psalm 110:3 The Bible (His story) employs the term "dew" in this sense in such verses as, declaring, that the people should follow only a king who was virile enough to be full of the "dew" His/his semen. (Hallelujah)

Solomon 2:3 In his shade I took great *delight* and sat down, and his fruit (semen) was sweet to my taste.

Solomon 5:2 I sleep, but my heart waketh: it is the voice of my beloved that knocketh, saying, Open to me, my sister, my love, my dove, my undefiled: for my head is filled with *dew*, and my locks (testicles) with the *dew* drops of the night.

Dew was once thought to be a sort of rain that fertilized the earth and, in time, became a metaphor for of men (Semen). The wife feeds her husband/mate who returns to her his/mate *dew*, the (man) *milk* (creator) of human kind. She keeps him healthy he keeps her healthy in body and spirit of love within in oneness. (his returning of **GOD**s making "semen thy creator" for her return in everlasting love)

This gift from **GOD** made within men is their semen, is His/his *sacrament* for her as for her to enjoy. A sacrament is a symbol which conveys divine grace, blessing, or sanctity upon the believer who participates in it, or a tangible symbol which represents an intangible reality. Generally accepted definition of a sacrament is that it is an outward sign that conveys an inward, spiritual grace. (wikipedia)

Psalm 4:2 How long, O men, will you turn my glory into shame? How long will you love delusions and seek false gods?

Psalm 14:2 The LORD looks down from heaven on the sons of men to see if there are any who understand, any who seek Him. (Sons that keep thy oath of tradition)

John 3:12 the author of the tractate intended that this was to be seen as symbolic of JESUS as the inner man, who had to be reached through the path of self knowledge, i.e.-"the kingdom of heaven is with you"." But seek His kingdom" for His/his kingdom is come within. John 5:17 Hitherto: [**GOD**s gift to men (semen) within you]

***NOTE: Semen is an anti-depressant, anti-anxiety and anti-ageing healing in studies women who consumed orally in tradition are replenished by this substance and sustained a better mood and were healthier. He also himself likewise took part as the provider of his semen, was not depressed or with anxiety and in a better mood and also a sleep aid unto both. (ref) (wikipedia)

Semen is a substance, blessed of **GODs** making, this that is flowing within men, bearings all that is vital to life and health to the spirit of love, is this glowing flowing within men is the utmost of their *essence*. To men their semen is there wealth, hidden treasure more precious than all rubies, gold or blood and **GOD** gave to men His/his purpose the ***upmost heights desire to shear of it regularly in tradition***.

The spiritual blessing within this like healing filled with power that throbs and spirit within men. A natural substance, this that gives life will continue her quality of life to her who enjoys of it. She/mate will be replenished men will be refreshed both are rerewarded. Follow the spiritual path, ***flee after him haply*** receive on appointed days and draw from him he well *haply of love* emanate that is made by **GOD** from within. (Ruth 2:9)   Let thine eyes be on the field that they do reap, and go thou after them: have I not charged the young men that they shall not touch thee? and when thou art athirst, go unto the vessels, and drink of that which the young men have drawn. (replenishing semen drawn from man is drink indeed)

Semen contains power that throbs is with healing, that is made by GOD, filled with testosterone, estrogen and other hormones full of minerals, high proteins, low-carb nutrients, and mood –altering chemicals that women need. Men have a well of made by GOD semen within them, sharing this will be a blessing and rerewarding to both is bliss. It is part of purpose for men to share of them self into her, as it is a blessing from GOD the father/creator.

Heb.2:14 Forasmuch then as the children are partakers of flesh and blood, He also Himself likewise took part of the same; that through death He might destroy him that had the power of death, that is, the devil; For in Him dwelleth all the fulness of the godhead bodily. (*Thy erect fullness of a Penis according to the fleshly kind*)

Tradition is the handing down of a belief in custom or practice, to stay in remembrance of a routine continually. For humans must seek his spirit to receive his blessing. **GOD** knowing this of us requires tradition and to be self-disciplined to seek him, in spirit of his making. In keeping of tradition this action with purpose is granted to us by the spiritual moment of his flowing semen. Tradition is the key to becoming a healing. Rejoice and enjoy with delight in life therefore fulfilling a part His and our purpose. Acts.2:30   Therefore being a prophet, and knowing that **GOD** had sworn with an oath to him, ***that of the fruit of his loins, according to the flesh***, he would raise up JESUS to sit on His throne.

As a man (husband / soul mate) I am to prepare my place within me. I am to stay strong in spirit of mind body and soul. Stay clean within and without of purpose of giving into her His/his making, this substance that He grants to me. For **GOD** has made this within me to continue into her, for her to be replenished in tradition on appointed days.

As a female (wife / soul mate) I am to prepare my place within me. I am to stay in strong spirit to receive into me of his making that **GOD** grants to me. For to me keep tradition *flee after him haply* on appointed days every flowing of his giving into me, for **GOD** has made this to continue into me from Him/him to replenish me in tradition on appointed days.

Without *timidity* through regular motivation and encouragement allow the spirit within ✝herapy plus of each *soul mate* to keep frequent flowing of His /his gift in tradition, enjoy the good spirit of sharing this beautiful gift. Do not waste His/his gift, as the capacity and need is to be develop and enjoyed of thy flowing semen, nurtured and encouraged by the spirit to keep thy tradition. *Do so,* ***the grater the spirit the grater thy beauty will come from within****. Remember thy days, to keep thy gift flowing* of man/soul mate that cometh of his semen. (The significance of two)

John 6:62 What if you were to see the Son of Man ascending where he was before? "that is when you witness the flowing of semen restored of its source"(The substance of the father, is restored to the son.) proclaims that the father is the eternal source of fullness of thy godhead bodily, from whom the son is begotten eternally, everlasting and also from whom the Holy Spirit proceeds (ascends/flowing/coming) eternally. (Eternal/everlasting, Fathers/living water/semen/creator is restored)

Isaiah 59:16 He saw that there was no one, he was appalled that there was no one to intervene; so his own arm worked *salvation* (orgasm) for him, and his own righteousness sustained him. (He masturbated and orally consumed himself) ***Wife / soul mate intervene, encourage your mate and assist him, thy spirit will be rerewarded.***

Seek, flee after find this gift within thy self, wife / soul mate intervene assist him add your spirit unto him in masturbating and enjoy with him drawing his substance from within him giving this gift with *delight* of what you love will bring you *delight* of love and love of *delight*. Seek the kingdom within his coming, with love for you his soul mates, love His/his gift from within. This that has come from within is now ***restored*** in tradition. (***The grater thy spirit the grater thy flowing***)

Deut. 11:27 Behold, A *blessing*, if ye obey the oath of the LORD, which I command you this day:

The power that throbs of the gift from **GOD**s love being given and received. We are responsible to each other, for each other and of each other what we give, receive and bring to each other. Everything **GOD** creates is good and all relative by spirit of life within each other from His *spirit within us,* there is love and life within each other. In this life, if we keep what we have within us this is our harvest. Letting go, that is our seed for the next harvest of semen. It takes two (one to give, one to receive) (one to be partaken of, one to be replenished by). This substance (semen), of **GOD**s making, that is within men, is all that is vital to life and health to the spirit, is this flowing within men is the utmost of His/his *essence*. A natural substance, this that gives life will continue quality of her life when she enjoys of it orally in tradition for ONLY GOOD COMES FROM GOOD HABITS**.** Both will be rerewarded by this as love within from **GOD**. Happiness isn't getting what you want it's enjoying what **GOD** will give you.

Women you cannot make yourself a more grateful or contented person, soul but you can ask for and seek it. (Matt.7:7) JESUS said: Ask, and it shall be given you; seek, and ye shall find; knock, and it shall be opened unto you. Open your mind body and soul to receive of **GOD**s love His/his gift for her to be given into her to fill her with delight, and His/his fruit is his sweet essence, of flowing living water his semen is *his return* for her delight within.

JOHN CHAPTER 1

1 ¶ In the beginning was the Word, and the Word was with GOD, and the Word was GOD.

2 The same was in the beginning with GOD.

3 All things were made by Him; and without Him/him was not anything made that was made.

4 In Him/him was life; and the life was the light of men. (semen/creator)

7 The same came for a witness, to bear witness of the Light, that all men through him might believe.

8 He was not that Light, but was sent to bear witness of that Light.

9 That was the true Light, which lighteth every man that cometh into the world.

13 Which were born, not of blood, nor of the will of the flesh, **nor of the will of man**, but of GOD. (Thy well of man within, semen/creator)

14 And the Word was made flesh, and dwelt among us, (and we beheld his glory, the glory as of the only begotten of the Father,) full of grace and truth.

LOVE OF LIFE AND THE LIFE OF
LOVE IS A GIFT OF HIS SEMEN.
(*The Love within*: there is none greater)

Luke 19:10 For the Son of man is come to seek and to save that which was lost. Let your manhood be a blessing to her; *rejoice* in thy wife/mate, she with love to draw and enjoy of your gift from GOD his sweet fruit of his loins. (For this is that part of which is lost)

Psalm 119:88. Preserve my **life** according to your **love**, and I will obey the statutes. Psalm 119:159

See how I **love** your precepts; preserve my **life**, O LORD, according to your **love**.

Ecclesiastes 9:9. *Enjoy **life** with your wife (soul mate)*, whom you **love,** all the days of this **life** that **GOD** has given you under the sun.

1Corin.11:3 It is written in the Bible, that a wife / soul mate be obedient to her husband /soul mate, and in *his return* of this, he should love her body as his own. Husband, submit to **GOD** and the wife / mate submits to the husband / mate.

Eph 5:14. Every once in a while we do wake up. And when we do, what we wake up to is gratitude for the things we take for granted.

Deut. 7:13 And He will love thee, and bless thee, and multiply thee: He will also *bless the fruit of thy womb*, and the fruit of thy land, thy corn, and thy wine, and thine oil, the increase of thy kine, and the flocks of thy sheep, in the land which he sware unto thy fathers to give thee.

John 6:54-64:

54 Whoso eateth my flesh, and drinketh my blood, hath eternal life; and I will raise him up at the last day.
55 For my flesh is meat indeed, and my blood is drink indeed.
56 He that eateth my flesh, and drinketh my blood, dwelleth in me, and I in him.
57 As the living Father hath sent me, and I live by the Father: so he that eateth me, even he shall live by me.
58 This is that bread which came down from heaven: not as your fathers did eat manna, and are dead: he that eateth of this bread shall live forever.

Father's Living Water 2

59 These things said he in the synagogue, as he taught in Capernaum.
60 ¶ Many therefore of his disciples, when they had heard this, said, This is an hard saying; who can hear it?
61 When JESUS knew in himself that his disciples murmured at it, he said unto them, Doth this offend you?
62 What and if ye shall see the Son of man ascend up where he was before?
63 It is the spirit that quickeneth; the flesh profiteth nothing: the words that I speak unto you, they are spirit, and they are life.
64 But there are some of you that believe not.

JESUS reveals himself as "the bread of life", telling the disbelieving disciples "it is not Moses who has given you the bread from heaven, but it is my Father who gives the true bread from heaven. The bread of life and living water of John's JESUS are present within himself. (His/his semen)

John 4:14-15 But whosoever drinketh of the water that I shall give him shall never thirst; but the water that I shall give him shall be in him a well of water springing up into everlasting life.
 15 The woman saith unto Him, Sir, give me this water, that I thirst not, neither come hither to draw. [Woman/soul mate draw from the well of your men's/soul mate living water (his semen) drinketh of the water, with love which he will springing up into you his love, to quench your athirst of His/his love now shall be within you everlasting life.](is restored)

"Living water" in this context refers to semen, which literally is the liquid of life. As JESUS indicates, drinking of the "living water" provides a spiritual replenishment for the soul. (Soul mates)

Halt im Gedächtnis **Jesum Christ** (*Hold in remembrance JESUS Christ*)

Chorus: Halt im Gedächtnis Jesum Christ - a lively chorus with words taken from 2 Timothy: 8 ¶ Remember that JESUS of the seed (semen) of David was raised from the dead on the **3rd** day according to my gospel. (do this in remembrance of me) (*Hold in remembrance Jesum Christ and restore him on the* **3rd** *day*)

John 2:19 JESUS answered and said unto them, Destroy this temple, and in three days I will raise it up. (restore/raised/Erect /erection/ resurrection)

JESUS so loved the world that He sacrifice himself for His faith of this action.

Matt. 20:15-16 So the last shall be first, and the first last: for many are called, but few are chosen.

Salvation in its nature must answer to the plight of humanity as it actually is. It must offer individuals redemption from slavery to sin, forgiveness from guilt, reconciliation for alienation and "renewal for a marred image of **GOD**".

The means of *salvation* are not well defined or understood. In common secular and scientific usage, "life" and "death" refer exclusively to the biological functions in an ***orgasm*** (The Highness in life/from heavens above, His/his is creation coming) (or lack thereof). The concept of both "life" and "death" are transcendent of biology—the human body may die, but the human being (i.e., mind, soul, self-concept) can live eternally, or else be dead. The soul, typically described as "the *essence* of a man being his (semen)," is thought to be transcendent and thus indicates a substantive link between human existence in a mortal human body and eternal life (soul). (Re-establishing a personal communion with GOD or sacrament) this salvation is a gift from GOD the Father that anyone may receive. (food for thy soul/mates)

Psalm 91:16 With long life will I satisfy him and show him my *salvation*.

Psalm 116:13 I will lift up the cup of *salvation* and call on the name of the LORD.

Psalm 40:16 But may all who seek you rejoice and be glad in you; may those who love your *salvation* always say, "The LORD be exalted!"

Isaiah 12:3 With joy thee well draw living water from thy *wells of salvation*.

Isaiah 45:8 "You heavens above, rain down righteousness; let the clouds shower it down. Let the earth open wide, let *salvation (semen)* spring up, let righteousness grow with it; I, the LORD, have created it. (Hallelujah)

Isaiah 59:16 He saw that there was no one, he was appalled that there was no one to intervene; so his own arm worked *salvation (orgasm)* for him, and his own righteousness sustained him. (He masturbated and orally consumed himself)

Isaiah 61:10 I delight greatly in the LORD; my soul rejoices in my GOD. For he has clothed me with garments of *salvation (orgasm)* and arrayed me in a robe of righteousness, as a bridegroom adorns his head like a priest, and as a bride adorns herself with her jewels. (Made of mans jewels / drops of semen)

(Romans 10:9-10) (Romans 10:13) Confession and believing: "If you declare with your mouth, 'JESUS is Lord,' and believe in your heart that **GOD** raised him from the dead on the 3rd day, you will be saved. For it is with your heart that you believe and are justified, and it is with your mouth that you profess your faith and are saved". "For whosoever shall call upon the name of the Lord shall be saved".

(Application of faith) (John 4:14 bless this living water and drink indeed)

Today's Churches of Christ reject what his faith is and call it original sin, *salvation* by faith alone. (Not the application of faith.)
(ref.)   wikipedia

Love: refers to a deep, ineffable feeling of tenderly caring for another person. Even this unlimited conception of love, encompasses a wealth of different feelings, from the passionate desire and intimacy of romantic love to feeling sexual emotional closeness.

The term *love* is to express your devotion to **GOD**. This love can be expressed by prayer, service, good deeds, and personal sacrifice. Reciprocally, **GOD** the Father loves all of His creation for GOD is love. (Fruit of the spirit) (Fruit of his loins) (Fruit of the womb)

Romance: the gift of sexuality is blessed by **GOD** the father when exercised within the bonds of marriage. Proverbs 5:18-19 "Let your manhood be a blessing; *rejoice* in the wife/mate of your youth. Let her charms and tender embrace satisfy you. Let her love alone fulfill her with your delight."

The Book of Babyalon 49: Thy tears, thy sweat, thy blood, thy semen, thy love, thy faith shall provide. Ah, ***I shall drain thee like the cup that is of me***. JESUS caught his own semen in order to demonstrate that such behavior was necessary for us to live by consuming his own flowing living water (semen).

Wife / soul mate the longer you let the lack of His/his gift from **GOD** not build up within you, the longer it will take to build up the enjoyment of this gift of power that throbs and energy within you that is within your husband/soul mate so build on this gift in tradition in appointed ways on appointed days. Your husband/ mate will renew your life and love life and sustain you with his love now within you.

For when a husband/mate gives from his body with spirit, into his wife/mate body from his body, then she is of his body in this spirit. For of this action (In Application of Faith) they become as one body of this spirit. Forasmuch his semen every drop of his making within belongs to Him/him.

His husband's & wife's (soul mates) become replenished and rerewarded in sharing of His/his making now within. (**Rejuvenation**)

"The Fruit of knowledge" (*Adam likewise a tree of his fruit with seed*)

Genesis 3:1 [*The Fall of Man from the grace of GOD*] Now the **serpent** was more crafty than any of the wild animals the LORD GOD had made. He said to the woman, "Did GOD really say, 'You must not eat from any tree in the garden'?"

Genesis 3:5 For GOD doth know that in the day ye eat thereof, then your eyes shall be opened, and ye shall be as gods, knowing ***good*** and evil.

3:6 And when the woman saw that the tree was ***good for food***, and that it was pleasant to the eyes, and a tree to be *desired to make one wise*, she took of the fruit thereof, and did eat, and gave also unto her husband with her; and he did eat.

The influence of ***manipulative power of suggestion*** (serpent/devil/satan/society/system/taboo) is saying to Eve that she is ***not to*** eat of his tree of sweet fruit. (The fruit of his loin) (The first of that which was lost) (Original offense: For her NOT to eat of His/his sweet fruit is an offense to Him) (Solomon 2:3) Like an apple tree among the trees of the forest is my lover among the young men. I delight to sit in his shade, and his fruit is sweet to my taste.

(John 6:54-64) and 2 Timothy: 8 ¶ Remember that JESUS was raised from the dead on the **3rd** day according to my gospel. (Do this in remembrance of me) (*Hold in remembrance Jesum Christ and restore him on the* **3rd** *day*)

Society's manipulative power of suggestion has put us in a box, we are aware of it. Instead we should be outside the box going with his glowing flowing of His spirit within. **GOD** provides for the woman / soul mate what she needs and the source of, his /soul mates sweet fruit (semen) for her to be *replenished* and for him to be *refreshed* of love by the gift from above. Wife / soul mate do not forsake your-self of your husband /soul mates gift, **GOD** made this gift of life for you, to be given into you to fill you with delight, this flowing living water his semen is delight. To men semen is there wealth, hidden treasure more precious than all rubies, gold or blood and **GOD** gave to men as part of his purpose the ***upmost heights desire to shear of it regularly in tradition on appointed days***. Why then is this gift that is made within men, rejected for whom it is made? John 6:61(Doth this offend you?) To Him/him, the rejection of this gift and love within and the giving of his flesh or Him/ him-self into his soul mate insults or offends Him/him the giver of this gift and the maker of this gift His/his semen. (The serpent/ evil/ devil wins)

Solomon 2:3 In his shade I took great *delight* and sat down, and his fruit was sweet to my taste. **Delight**: Means happiness and may refer to someone or something that brings such a state of delight, such as good-tasting food. (Sweet fruit/semen)

For as he walks in this world of light, he will cast no shadow, for **GODs** light is within. A bright candle of habit thee will be, day by day, delight to delight. With delight in mind is truly where he will be, with **GODs** light showing way of good habits and his returning for her delight. *Rejoice with your wife/mate for her delight*; enjoy life in tradition of good habits. *Hold in remembrance Jesum Christ and restore/erection of him,* it's of purpose. (Delight is part of your purpose)

John 12:36 While Ye have delight, believe in delight, that ye may be the children of delight.

(Galatians 5:19-23) The fruit of the Spirit is: *love, joy, peace, patience, kindness, goodness, faithfulness, gentleness and self-control*. To keep a Covenant (oath): Tradition on appointed days.

JESUS the only begotten (to bread forward) son of GOD; the author of Ecclesiasticus, a book of the Apocrypha (seed / star of David) (without sin unto His Father nor the laws of men) our severer of that what was lost in the beginning "the first sin". (LORD / Master / Messias / presence of peace / rock/ prophet / teacher/ vassal / mediator / from whom all blessing (happiness) flow) the light and the way of all Righteousness of delight (fruit of the spirit / spirit within / love / seed /fruit / living water / pearls /wine / kingdom / substance / essence / healing / faith / grace / salvation / the bread of life / the gift from above / everlasting / giver of Himself / casted out demons) of the soul within. Messiah means literally; covered in oil, anointed. Therefore all these.... exist not for its own pleasure or purpose. It must flow into a vassal other than itself; only then does it fulfill its purpose. For in Him dwelleth all the fullness of the godhead bodily. (*Thy restored erect Penis according to the fleshly kind with fullness of the gift of life from within*)

Symbols: Something that stands for or represents another thing.

This was the symbol for JESUS before his death.

Fish swim in water or the liquid of life and are consumed or eaten. Seminal fluid produced by male fish. (living water as food to drink indeed)

Tantric: A man offering his semen through masturbator for consumption from a cup, these practices was referred to as a "fish", a symbol of the living JESUS. (Ref. sacredsemen)

(Matthew 4:19) (Mark 1:16-18) As JESUS walked beside the Sea of Galilee, he saw Simon and his brother Andrew casting a net into the lake, for they were fishermen. "Come, follow me," JESUS said, "and I will make you fishers of men." At once they left their nets and followed him. (Fisher: one that partakers of flesh of "fish")

John 4:14 But whosoever drinketh of the water that I shall give him shall never thirst; but the water that I shall give him shall be in him a well of water springing up into everlasting life.

John 4:36 And he that reapeth receiveth wages, and gathereth fruit unto life eternal: that both he that soweth and he that reapeth may rejoice together.
37 And herein is that saying true, One soweth, and another reapeth. John 6:54-58
54 Whoso eateth my flesh, and drinketh my blood, hath eternal life; and I will raise him up at the last day.
55 For my flesh is meat indeed, and my blood is drink indeed.

56 He that eateth my flesh, and drinketh my blood, dwelleth in me, and I in him.
57 As the living Father hath sent me, and I live by the Father: so he that eateth me, even he shall live by me.
58 This is that bread which came down from heaven: not as your fathers did eat manna, and are dead: he that eateth of this bread shall live forever.

This is the symbol for JESUS after his death. JESUS so loved the world that He sacrifice Himself for His application of His faith. (Martyr)

This particular understanding of sin, as a form of debt that humanity inherits, is related to the soteriological theory of substitutionary atonement, which states that JESUS died on the cross as a propitiation, or substitute, for sinners.

Genesis 3:1 In the Beginning (The first Original offense) John 6:61(Doth this offend you?)

Heb.2:14 Forasmuch then as the children are partakers of flesh and blood, He also Himself likewise took part of the same; that through death He might destroy him that had the power of death, that is, the devil; For in Him dwelleth all the fulness of the godhead bodily. (*Behold thy resurrection with fullness of the gift of life, thy Penis according to the fleshly kind*)

(Romans 10:9-10) (Romans 10:13) Confession and believing: "If you declare with your mouth 'JESUS is LORD,' and believe in your heart that **GOD** raised (resurrected/restored) Him from the dead on the 3rd day, you will be saved. For it is with your heart that you believe and are justified, and it is with your mouth that you profess your faith and are saved". (Works, the application of faith to behold)

2 Timothy: 8 Remember that JESUS Christ of the seed (semen) of David was raised (resurrected) from the dead (restored) on the **3rd** day according to my gospel.

John 6:56 He that eateth my flesh, and drinketh my blood, dwelleth in me, and I in him. John 6:54-64 Follow His gospel (do this in remembrance of me)

John 5:17 Hitherto: change in which individuals of a species mature past adulthood and take on unseen traits. [**GOD**s gift to men (semen) within]

(Mark 2:17) (Matthew 5:6, Matthew 6:33) **JESUS** (The Master) came to the world to address the needs, not of "the righteous", but of "sinners". Righteousness, like the Kingdom of Heaven, is **GOD**s gift to men (semen) through grace.

    Perplexing yet so simple and in the land of thy fathers semen has given thee, as why after all the proof both in the Bible and science of manifesting of healing power of Semen Aloe Prayer (SAP) as why the world has lack of knowledge and application of faith in this part of **GOD the Father** purpose for and of His kingdom. Instead we should be following His gospel flowing with glowing His flowing of the spirit within. Everything **GOD** has created is good, full of His blessing (happiness) and spirit within of His love. Adam he is in you as you are of him. The fall from **GOD**s grace the serpent/devil/satan/society/system/taboo) (The box influence) has taken the love of life and the life of love of His/his purpose. [Father; allow us to rejoice of each other in love of this flowing gift to us through your grace the gift from above of His/his kingdom from within thy gifts.] AMEN

For the spirit within these words live, believe and receive within the application of faith, save that which was lost, follow His gospel. Praise GOD from whom all blessing flow. ***For action of love with spirit speaks greater than words***.

Forasmuch as a secret is not a secret until you hide it. Forasmuch of ***all*** these are not a secret. (Them That Know" KNOW") *Rejoice with your wife/soul mate*; enjoy life in his returning on the appointed days for her delight with tradition of good habits. It's part of GODs purpose and ours now restored.

Luke 19:10 Chief of these writings: he that doth serve, to dedicate this writings to our LORD and MASTER. To keep thy Covenant: oath of tradition on appointed days. LORD, grant unto your servants to (restore) save that which was lost and the wisdom to know the way of this that part was lost. (Master, we as soul mates are part of your purpose, keep us wholly and flowing with love from within our souls and body)

(Matthew 7: 15-20) (Deut. 18:21-22) The reception of a message is termed revelation; the delivery of the message is termed prophecy. For Christians the authenticity of a prophet is judged as JESUS said; that one should judge a prophet, by his fruits. (His/his fruit)

(Acts.2:30) Therefore being a son of man, and knowing that **GOD** had sworn with an ***oath*** to Him," ***that of the fruit of his loins, according to the flesh"*** do declare, to keep thy oath. To lift up thy cup of *salvation* within the application of faith,(restore) save that which was lost.(Resurrection) HIS all will not be lost when all will remember His Cross in the sky that drop down Dew. AMEN

Luke19:10 For the Son of man is come to seek and to save that which was lost.

Colossians 4:14 One of JESUS' disciples was a physician named "Luke" whom the Bible says was also "beloved" as a disciple of JESUS.

Complementary benefits within thy gifts from GOD the Fathers Living Waters

What are considered complementary or alternative practices in one country may be considered conventional medical practices in another. Therefore, the definition is broad and general: complementary medicine includes all such practices and ideas which are outside the domain of conventional medicine in several countries and defined by its users as preventing or treating illness, or promoting health and well-being. These practices complement mainstream medicine by 1: contributing to a common whole, 2: satisfying a demand not met by conventional practices (The box influence), and 3: diversifying the conceptual framework of medicine.

No pill will do for you like the power from within His/his semen can do within you. He supplies you both as mates, with what you need and the source of it.
(The significance of two)

Hormones testosterone: benefits within semen

Testosterone is one of the hormones controlling libido in human beings. Research is showing that hormonal contraception methods like "the pill" (which rely on estrogen and progesterone together) are causing low libido in females by elevating levels of Sex Hormone Binding Globulin. SHBG binds to sex hormones, including testosterone, rendering them unavailable. Research question whether "the pill" and other hormonal methods have permanently altered gene expression by epigenetic mechanisms. (*Women enjoy this gift from Him/him **NOT** "the pill".*)

Left untreated, women with low testosterone levels will experience loss of libido which in turn can often cause *relationship stress* and loss of bone and muscle mass throughout their lives. (Low testosterone may also be responsible for certain kinds of depression and low energy states.) Women /soul mate; why let the lack of this gift, get you in a bad mood and take it out on him / soul mate, when he has a gift within from above that the enjoying of his flowing giving will cure you both of this stress. Keep His/his gift flowing as drink indeed, fresh and alive and your love of life and life of love well be also.

Conversely, increasing testosterone from regular oral consumption of semen generally has a positive correlation with libido in both sexes.

Libido in its common usage means sexual desire are more general, referring to libido as the free creative-or psychic-energy an individual has to put toward personal development or individuation.

Testosterone is a steroid hormone from the androgen group. In humans, testosterone is primarily secreted in the testes of males and the ovaries of females, although small amounts are also secreted by the adrenal glands. It is the principal male sex hormone and an anabolic steroid.

In men, testosterone plays a key role in health and well-being as well as in osteoporosis. On average, an adult human male body produces about forty to sixty times more testosterone than an adult female body, but females are, from a *behavioral perspective*, more sensitive to the hormone.

The three major naturally occurring estrogens in women are estrone, estradiol, and estriol. Estradiol is the predominate form in nonpregnant females, estrone is produced during menopause, and estriol is the primary estrogen of pregnancy. In the body these are all produced from androgens through actions of enzymes.

From menarche to menopause the primary is estrogen. In postmenopausal women more estrone is present than estradiol. Estradiol is produced from testosterone by aromatase and estrone from androstenedione within the female that she / soul mate needs to be replenished from the male/soul mate. Premarin, a commonly prescribed estrogenic *"drug"*(**not** from men) contains the steroidal estrogens equilin and equilenin, in addition to estrone sulfate but *due to its health risk*, more *genetic* estrogen Progynova are now more often prescribed by doctors. (The box influence)

Estrogens: benefits within semen

The male body produces about forty to sixty times more *testosterone* than an adult female body. (Humen / Women / Semen / Ah-men / AMEN)

Estrogens are a group of steroid compounds, named for their importance in the estrous cycle, and functioning as the primary female sex hormone. Some estrogens are also produced in smaller amounts by other tissues such as the liver, adrenal glands, and the breasts. These secondary sources, semen for estrogens are especially important in postmenopausal women.

Estrogen is considered to play a significant role in women's mental health. A sudden estrogen withdrawal, fluctuating estrogen, and periods of sustained estrogen low levels correlated with significant mood lowering. Women recovery from depression postpartum, perimenopause, and postmenopause was shown to be effective after levels of estrogen from regular oral consumption of semen were stabilized and/or restored.

Hormone b**enefit**: within semen

Hormone replacement from oral consumption of semen regularly, women received estrogen and other hormones, and to postmenopausal women in order to prevent osteoporos*is* as well as treat the symptoms of menopause such as hot flashes, vaginal dryness, urinary stress incontinence, chilly sensations, dizziness, fatigue, irritability, sweating and mood swings with loss of libido with low energy states.

Fractures of the spine, wrist, and hips decrease by 50-70% and spinal bone density increases by 5% in those women treated in the same manner within 3 years of the onset of menopause and 5 to15 years thereafter.

Hormones have the following effects on the body: stimulation or inhibition of growth mood swings induction or suppression of apoptosis (programmed cell death) activation or inhibition of the immune system regulation of metabolism preparation of the body for fighting, sex, fleeing, mating, and other activity preparation of the body for a new phase of life, such as puberty, parenting, and menopause control of the reproductive cycle hunger cravings. A hormone may also regulate the production and release of other hormones. Hormone signals control the internal environment of the body through homeostasis. (wikipedia.org/wiki/)

Other benefits: within semen

Semen is primarily protein and minerals such as zinc and calcium. Semen has 5 to 7 calories per teaspoon. Research has shown that semen is a powerful organic antidepressant because of epinephrine and various mood-altering hormones that it contains, and it has thus been called, *"Nature's Prozac for women."*

Seminophagia provides the body with testosterone, which is important to maintain muscle and bone strength. While women need a smaller proportion of testosterone than men, it is just as important to female health as it is to male. Testosterone reduces the risk *of heart attack, protects against stroke*, and can treat *diabetes.*

In addition, there are three published studies with findings indicating that semen consumption orally is able to prevent *breast cancer.* This effect is attributed to its glycoprotein and selenium content.

Seminophagia's greatest benefit may be the fact that semen contains a substance which conditions a mother's immune system to accept the "foreign" proteins found in sperm as well as the resulting fetus and placenta, keeping blood pressure low and thereby reducing the risk of preeclampsia. Regular consumption to the baby's father's semen, especially orally, helps make a woman's pregnancy safer and more successful, because she is absorbing her partner's / soul mates antigens.

Chemical barriers also protect against infection. The skin and respiratory tract secrete antimicrobial peptides such as the ß-defensins. Enzymes such as lysozyme and phospholipase A2 in saliva, tears, and breast milk are also antibacterials.
Vaginal secretions serve as a chemical barrier following menarche, when they become slightly acidic, while semen contains defensins and zinc to kill pathogens. In the stomach, gastric acid and proteases serve as powerful chemical defenses against ingested pathogens.

Disorders in the immune system can result in disease. Immunodeficiency diseases occur when the immune system is less active than normal, resulting in recurring and life-threatening infections.

Immunodeficiency can either be the result of a genetic disease, such as severe combined immunodeficiency, or be produced by pharmaceuticals or an infection, such as the acquired immune deficiency syndrome (AIDS) that is caused by the retrovirus HIV. In contrast, autoimmune diseases result from a hyperactive immune system attacking normal tissues as if they were foreign organisms. Common autoimmune diseases include *Hashimoto's Thyroiditis, rheumatoid arthritis, diabetes mellitus type 1 and lupus* erythematosus. Immunology covers the study of all aspects of the immune system which has significant relevance to human health and diseases.

Nutritional value: *food* within semen

Semen is primarily composed of water and Hormones, but has been shown to contain trace amounts of virtually every nutrient the human body uses. It has somewhat higher amounts of commonly deficient minerals such as potassium, magnesium and selenium. One typical flowing contains 150 mg of protein, 11 mg of carbohydrates, 6 mg fat, 3 mg cholesterol, 7% US RDA potassium and 3% US RDA copper and zinc. When metabolized, protein yields 4 kcal/g, carbohydrate also yields 4 kcal/g, and fat yields 9 kcal/g. Hence the food energy in the typical ejaculation or flowing is 0.7 kcal/g (2.9 kJ) within. (***Living water (semen) is, food and medicine as drink indeed*** and spiritual replenishment for *soul mates*) (ref) Wikipedia

A dietary supplement within semen

✝herapy plus for women / wife /soul mate a natural and supernatural power, preventive for soul mates benefit will lower thy chances of weight increasing of thy body for your rereward within His/his replenishing living waters (semen/aloe) is food and Madison as beautiful drink indeed. A dietary supplement, also known as food supplement or nutritional supplement, is a preparation intended to provide nutrients, such as vitamins and minerals. *"Nature's slim-fast for women."*

Preventing Loss of Love (long suffering)

Soul mates can take action within thy application of thy faith will prevent losing thy gift of GODs love. Enjoy flowing of His/his gifts twice a weak within the application faith of keeping thy substance fresh for soul mates. Keep love alive and thy semen/aloe fresh all within tradition. Keep strong His/his gifts flowing, fresh, alive and your *love of life and life of love* well be also.

✝herapy plus for men / soul mate keep thy fruit (semen) sweet and full of spiritual energy consume more low-fat, high-fiber foods, or foods with omega-3 fatty acids, such as: Soy products, like tofu and soy beans, Fish, like salmon, albacore tuna. Drink Aloe juice twice a week: red wine or green tea and supplements: such as vitamins D and E, Zink, Ginkgo Biloba, Calcium and Pineapple juice (NOT from Concentrate). Red foods like tomatoes, beets and foods that contain tomato. Vegetables like broccoli, cauliflower. Other foods like walnuts, peanut butter, flaxseed-oil, Bee Pollen, black olives, cinnamon and honey. Men / soul mate for both soul mates keep thy semen healthy consume these in tradition.

Keep thy self clean and fresh and alive within and without, with purpose of thy giving with love within thy substance, wealth of all within thy sweet fruit thy beautiful gift that is granted you as a *gift* from Him/him whom all bliss flows.

Avoiding other food like dairy (ice cream) Red meats or eating less of them is a major prevention of cancer. *Thy wife / soul mate feed your husband / mate well.*

Zinc is a metal. It is called an "essential trace element" because very small amounts of zinc and calcium are necessary for human health consume them in tradition. How does it work? Zinc is needed for the proper growth and maintenance of the human fleshly body. Zinc is needed for immune function, wound healing, blood clotting, thyroid function, and much more.

†herapy plus will improve survival of soul mates through the immune system in the fight against this cancer within men and women. †herapy plus reduces the risk *of heart attack, protects against stroke, Brest and prostate cancer* and can *even treat diabetes, stress and low libido within soul mates.*
(**What a beautiful gift indeed to drink twice a week**)

While acknowledging that †herapy plus is an important cancer prevention treatment. Soul mates in *tradition* of †herapy plus; live longer, have happier love lives in bliss on average, than others not knowing of this wisdom.

Active ✝herapy plus consisting of given/receiving over the course of therapy; side effects were wild; consisting mainly of bliss-like symptoms that improved greatly within a few therapy treatments. *Rejoice with your soul mate*; enjoy life and love its part of our purpose.

Natural Hormone Therapy for Cancer Preventive

Natural hormone therapy means removing, blocking, or adding hormones to fight cancers. Knowledge about cancer and hormones within ✝herapy plus is the gift from above of His wisdom within Fathers living waters.

✝herapy plus is the therapy that is right. This therapy is found to be reasonably safe and effective for over 2,000 years plus. ✝herapy plus is His/his *wealth, this gift is for soul mate's health in sharing.*

✝herapy plus within **Aloe** a natural and supernatural power, many substance are a healing in treating disease, preventive, curing and improving with preserving health. It's all filled with goodness. One of many GODs living waters for health to drink, Spirit in liquid substance is drink indeed as food / health. The **Aloe** *Vera*: A natural medicine for cancer, cholesterol, diabetes, inflammation, IBS, and other health conditions. This gift is for soul mate's health each drink 1or 2 oz. twice weak.

Numbers 24:6
"Like valleys they spread out, like gardens beside a river, like **aloe**s planted by the LORD, like cedars beside the waters.

Psalm 45:8
All your robes are fragrant with myrrh and **aloe**s and cassia; from palaces adorned with ivory the music of the strings makes you glad.

Proverbs 7:17
I have perfumed my bed with myrrh, **aloe**s and cinnamon.

Song of Solomon 4:13-15 Thy plants are an orchard of pomegranates, with pleasant fruits; camphire, with spikenard,
14 Spikenard and saffron; calamus and cinnamon, with all trees of frankincense; myrrh and **aloes**, with all the chief spices:
15 ¶ A fountain of gardens, a well of living waters, and streams from Lebanon.

John 19:39 He was accompanied by Nicodemus, the man who earlier had visited JESUS at night. Nicodemus brought a mixture of myrrh and **aloes**, about seventy-five pounds

- Halts the growth of cancer tumors.
- Lowers high cholesterol.
- Repairs "sludge blood" and reverses "sticky blood".
- Boosts the oxygenation of your blood.
- Eases inflammation and soothes arthritis pain.
- Protects the body from oxidative stress.
- Prevents kidney stones and protects the body from oxalates in coffee and tea.
- Alkalizes the body, helping to balance overly acidic dietary habits.
- Cures ulcers, IBS, Crohn's disease and other digestive disorders.
- Reduces high blood pressure natural, by treating the cause, not just the symptoms.
- Nourishes the body with minerals, vitamins, enzymes and glyconutrients.

- Accelerates healing from physical burns and radiation burns.
- Replaces dozens of first aid products, makes bandages and antibacterial sprays obsolete.
- Halts colon cancer, heals the intestines and lubricates the digestive tract.
- Ends constipation.
- Stabilizes blood sugar and reduces triglycerides in diabetics.
- Prevents and treats candida infections.

The health and nutrition benefits within Aloe vera juice, and Aloe vera gel for the skin, are long time legend. Most humans know first-hand the soothing relief of Aloe vera gel on minor burns and cuts! But did you know that *drinking* Aloe vera juice provides your body with 200 health promoting compounds, including 20 minerals, 18 amino acids and 12 vitamins. Aloe Vera Juice is favored by those looking to maintain a healthy digestive system and a natural energy level with optimum health and nutrition. You probably already know how great Aloe vera is for your skin. Did you also know Aloe vera is one of many vitamin and mineral-packed nutrition drink you can enjoy in His making within! Many humans drink Aloe vera gel as well as use it on their skin, gums, hair and scalp, for a number of reasons. Aloe is for Energy, Immune Function and Support, Digestion, Skin Regeneration, and more. Aloe Barbadensis miller is the type of aloe used in most commercial products with aloe vera content available today. Aloe vera juice drinks are made only from barbadensis miller for optimum nutrition and good health benefits within.

Mingling: ✝herapy **Plus** brings together in combination, without loss of individual characteristics. Found to be reasonably safe and effective for over 2,000 years plus, *regular oral* *consumption of semen and aloe is natural and supernatural healing drink indeed.*

> ✝herapy plus for *soul mates.* A Covenant (oath): Tradition on appointed days.
> (Wisdom in Application of Faith)

Acts.2:30) Therefore being a prophet, and knowing that **GOD** had sworn with an oath to him, *that of the fruit of his loins, according to the flesh*, he would raise up **JESUS** to sit on His throne. **JESUS**, the mediator of this covenant (**oath**); enjoyed by all in **JESUS**. (Deut. 11:27) Behold, A *blessing when,* ye *obey the oath of the LORD* which I command you this day. (Isaiah 45:8) Drop down ye heavens, from above, and let the skies pour down righteousness: let the earth open, and let them bring forth salvation, and let righteousness spring up together; I the Lord have created it.

Semen Aloe Prayer (SAP)

LORD and Master given unto me "Wisdom" as a man (husband / soul mate) I am to prepare my place within me to keep thy fruit sweet. I am to stay strong in the spirit of mind body and soul. Stay clean within, drink juice of Aloe, thy Sacred plant ,twice a week and keep clean thy source with purpose of giving into you thy mate, His making, this substance thy semen His gift within me that He grants to me. For **GOD the Father created** this within me to continue into you my soul mate, for you in return to be replenished in tradition. For behold; dwelleth all the fullness from within thy godhead bodily. ("Pray, O LORD, bless this living water") as it flows from within me, to bless you/my mate that receives thy gift of love and life and life of love in delight.

As a female (wife / soul mate) I am to prepare my place within me, for I have "Wisdom" of drinking His/his sacred gifts

twice a week of the goodness within for me. I am to stay strong in the Spirit of giving/receiving into me of His/his making that He grants to me. For to me keep tradition on appointed days for every flowing of His/his giving into me, for He/he has made this to continue into me. The best things in life are natural and free to be free from disease and long suffering. Therefore, the same substance that creates life, His semen, is also saving lives that it created. Consumed orally, from his source is promoting good health in the female, soul mate. Of flesh and Spirit; a beautiful drink to replenish thee.

Seek His kingdom within; with love for both soul mates, love His gifts from within. This that has come from within is now restored in tradition. (***The greater thy spirit the greater the offering of thy flowing gifts***) (The significance of two)

Rejoice let go and enjoy of spirit within a journey with His/his sacred gifts given/receiving ***twice a week*** in tradition. We His *soul mates* will obey the "OATH" keep in tradition on appointed days by the spirits ***haply flee after thy spirit of sharing to Mingle Semen Aloe Prayer.*** Seek of His Spirit within the gifts of His glowing flowing. We (husband /wife / soul mate) sealed this ***oath*** with a kiss of LOVE).
Free Spirits/Soul Mates Amen

Seek His kingdom and His righteousness, and all these things will be given to you. (His kingdom is within; His will be done on earth as it is heaven.)

Ecclesiastes 9:9. *Enjoy life with your wife (soul mate)*, whom you love, all the days of this life that **GOD** has given you under the sun.

EVERLASTING LOVE OF LIFE AND THE LIFE OF LOVE OF HIS GIFTS
(There is none greater than thy Creator)

EVERLASTING
Love grows when living water (semen) flows

This flowing from *everlasting* is filled with **GODs** *love* in spirit within His making. This of goodness that is His, forasmuch every drop of His/his making within belongs to Him. Semen a *gift* from GOD of whom all bliss flows is His/his.

With this comes truth: the glory of **JESUS** is the fullness of grace, glory and truth. In that He is the truth and the delight within himself, is a vassal of love for *his return* to us; He is LORD and MASTER of all His glory within His kingdom and righteousness and *everlasting love is His/his flow coming from within.*

Semen is living water the juice that circulates/flowing through a man His/his sweet fruit, is vital to life within men is hidden wealth of this gift is for our health. We prosper, when we are nurtured by His/his living wealth. This spirit is within (S+A+P) and thus, we are replenished and rerewarded. (John 4-14: Living water (semen) is spiritual replenishment for the soul)

Numbers 24-6: Like valleys, they spread out like gardens beside a river, like aloe planted by the LORD, like cedars beside the waters of life. (Living water)

The **A***loe Vera*: A natural medicine for cancer, cholesterol, diabetes, inflammation, IBS, and other health conditions.

Deut. 11-27: Behold, A *blessing when,* ye *obey the oath of the LORD* which I command you this day. (In Application of thy Faith)

John 6: JESUS said: For my flesh is meat indeed and my blood is drink indeed. His/his well of living water (semen/flesh) wealth for health, to drink indeed.

Genesis 3:6 And when the woman saw that his tree was *good for food*, and that it was pleasant to her eyes, and his tree of fruit be desired, she took of his fruit thereof, and did eat, and gave also unto her husband; and he did eat.

Mingling of love and life: Significances of Two ="One Love Within"

Living Water ✝**herapy Plus** this natural healings combined within (Semen Aloe Prayer) by regular oral consumption of this *mingling* promotes a natural health flesh, love and spiritual life. We as *soul mates* will this and show this as truth with no shadow. We as *soul mates* are witness of His truth and glory within His gifts. (Significance of Two in Application of our Faith)

✝herapy Plus for ***Husband and Wife*** (*soul mates each in sharing*) (SAP) = (1-complete fresh flowing of **S**emen) (**A**loe) (1/2 each of S+A) drink indeed.

1- Wife (*Soul Mate*) Draw/flow from your soul mate his making into a glass bowl or offering cup that is now of his glowing flowing with thy works. Rejoice of him letting it all flow, this is giving of love and his gift is for our harvest, *keep these gifts fresh*. (*Rejoice* of this *gift* from GOD of whom all blessing flow)

Note: Upon emanating his flowing gift of semen from GOD into the offering cup, he Prays: "***O LORD Bless this living water***" as it flows from within him.

Lift up this offering cup of thy Gift of thy Semen now within this cup.

2- *Mingle* the Aloe with his semen within the offering cup.

To be consumed within the moment of *mingling*. Upon drinking of this offering cup: Toast to thy Master and both pray **"O LORD Bless these living waters"** and drinketh of these living waters of love and life with *delight* from GOD to be *replenished and refreshed*, be healed by these gifts from above with delight.

John 4-37: And herein is that saying true, One soweth, and another reapeth. That both he that soweth and he that reapeth may rejoice together.

Living Water †herapy Plus is a Covenant: We His *soul mates* will obey the oath keep strong in tradition on appointed days by the spirits, ***haply flee after thy spirit of sharing and to Mingle*** Semen, Aloe and Prayer. Seek of His spirit within these gifts in flowing as a beautiful gift to drink indeed. (In Application of our Faith) with Lord JESUS, the mediator of this oath; enjoyed by all in JESUS. (LORD and Master)   AMEN

Isaiah 45:8 You heavens above, rain down righteousness; let the clouds shower it down. (*dew* drops)

(There is none greater than His love and life from within His gifts)

Thy wife soul mate feeds her husband / soul mate healthy foods he returns to his soul mate his dew/semen/creator "the (man) milk of human kind". She keeps him healthy he keeps her healthy in body and spirit of love within in oneness. His glowing flowing gift from above of living water is what GOD gives to us as beautiful, wonderful and free has become replaced with many illusions or deceptions causing more problems than solutions. By tradition our ancestors cured themselves of disease and long suffering. Therefore everything **GOD** has created is good, full of His blessing and spirit within and has definite purpose. (the gift of love and life and life of love)

GOD's gift, semen is the giver of all life and cause of all living creation. In cultures His/his gift is worshiped as an erect penis and in festivals. In the New Testament gospel of St.John it is said that in the beginning was the "word" or in Greek the "Logus." This refers to the life giving semen coming from the top of thy erect (erection) Sacred Mount or full penis. The custom is an old one that is connected to bringing about a good harvest of semen/creation. (Gen.3:6 In the beginning was the word, **GOD** said it is good for food and the word become flesh from within and (john 6:61) JESUS said "eateth my flesh") as drink indeed.

The moment we rediscovered our self, **GOD** reappeared in our life. We no longer have to prove or explain, we praise **GOD**. We only have to experience **GOD**, which makes our life and our love even more rich and beautiful. It's wonderful to believe in a beautiful, true **GOD**. It provides hope and inspiration and gives our life a deeper meaning. When we *let go* of our blind faith, more space was created within us for spiritual experiences. A head full of facts and details was no longer standing in the way, which allowed the heart and to speak to the soul. Letting go was the best thing that could have happened to us, because now we believe again. Letting go of it all is getting *closer to far away* where **JESUS** lives within the light of delight the stillness not that far away for our delight. There is where all can be found. The glowing flowing of the spirit within living water (semen) is thy flesh within men as in oneness. Special thanks: Wholly Spirits in Oneness within Lord JESUS.

The Illusionist

BY: Matthew E. Powers

Shuffle, Shuffle,
Spread and Dribble,
The hands of a master
Performing a riffle

Manipulation of cards,
And when his hand glides,
It comes to the top
And flips on its sides.

They say it's a miracle,
He knows it's not
They stare with blank faces
Then explodes like a shot

He looks at them and smiles
They ask where it went,
Reality transformed,
Their perceptions: bent

Cheating the impossible
The people crazed,
Their minds contorted,
Confused, amazed

So if he looks in your direction,
Or walks your way
Ask for wonder
Ask for magic
Ask the Illusionist
To play.

Fine Pearl's

Pearl's: Such an idea would certainly throw a new light on JESUS' had he revealed this secret Gnostic- Tantric technique of ingesting semen (pearls) at one of his sermons before Jewish crowds!

Matthew 7:6 Do not give dogs what is sacred; do not throw your pearls to pigs. If you do, they may trample them under their feet, and then turn and tear you to pieces.

Matthew 13:45 Again, the kingdom of heaven is like a merchant looking for fine pearls.

1 Timothy 2:9 I also want women to dress modestly, with decency and propriety, **not** with braided hair or gold or pearls (of oysters) or expensive clothes. (She to grace herself with the Fine *Pearls of man*)

Revelation 21:21 The twelve gates were twelve *pearls*, each gate made of a single *pearl*. The great street of the city was of pure gold, like transparent glass. (Living water / semen)

Prov. 3:22 So shall they be life unto thy soul, and grace to thy neck.
(The Fine Pearls of man)

The Pearly gates in, is an informal name for the gateway to Heaven. The image of the gates in popular culture is a set of large, white or wrought-iron gates in the clouds, guarded by Saint Peter (the keeper of the "key to the kingdom") (refers to a erect penis that brings forth the fine *Pearls of man His/his semen*)

THY SELF

Question: Do you know thy self? Who and what thy self is? Do you have what there is no law against you to have, within you? (*Fruit of the Spirit*) (Your soul / thy self is within)

Self- realization: Complete fulfillment of thy self.

Self- renunciation: Desires toward the benefit of others.

Self- serving: Supplying self with what is needed. (Within sharing)

Self-control: To keep seeking good traditions or habits. (Works, the application of faith) Believe in yourselves, for that is what brings you to your everlasting beauty.

Seek and find thy self (self-awareness), love of one's self before you can love others. Love the spirit of thy self. Draw of thy self from within thy self. Lift up thy self and love what the spirit has given into you within. Share all the love that thy self have within, if you keep what you have within, that is not sharing your love, rejoice in loving thy self as you will love in giving of thy self to receive. How can you love if you do not love that which comes of thy self, that which is from within thy self. Love what you give unto others of thy self this is the gift of all within love. When you love that what you give, that is a gift of love from thy self. (Against such things there is no law) (Gal. 5:19-23)

Seek and find this gift within thy self, draw that what is within thy self and give that gift with *delight* of that what you love this gift will bring *delight* of love and love of *delight*. Seek the kingdom within and show that this is that witch that you love.

Offer this gift from within of love, there is none grater, than the gift of love from within, giving of this gift is now made complete. Forasmuch he that not knowing of this love can't give this love. This is not love of thy self; this is the love of what is given unto you to love, love this gift and the giving of this gift from within thy self and thy self will receive love in return unto to thy self. (Significance of Two) (Within sharing love from within thy self) (There is none greater than LOVE)

The Book of Babylon 49: Thy tears, thy sweat, thy blood, thy living water, love, thy faith shall provide unto thy self and others. (Everlasting love flowing into everlasting love)

(Luke 17:20-21) JESUS as the inner man, who had to be reached through the path of self knowledge "the kingdom of heaven is with you" (Seek yea this kingdom within thy self)

Soul Mates Prayer: Lord, show us the feeling of your love, we know you're out there, you know we are here all of your spirits are so pretty, all of your spirits are so happy. Spirits take us with you, *let us go and enjoy your flowing into us, into your making and feeling all the love within.* For of your spirits flowing will add into us as your making within. Lord, your spirit within living waters quinces the fire of want and need within our passion. Of all things given unto us of your love, ***we give our thankfulness to you Lord in advance***. For that all He giveth; for only He can take away. (Significance of Two) AMEN

Everlasting

This is filled with fathers *love* in spirit within His making. This gift of goodness that is His forasmuch every drop of His making within belongs to Him / him.

As a *gift* from GOD of whom all bliss flows *his return.* ✝herapy Plus for *soul mates* (Significance of Two) Thankfulness: Wholly Spirits in Oneness

A gift from above from above, all bliss flows His/*his return is everlasting.*

Forasmuch as a secret is not a secret until you hide it. Forasmuch of all these are not a secret. (Them That Know" KNOW")

Serenity Prayer

GOD grant me the serenity to accept the things I can not change, Courage to change the things that I can and the wisdom to know the difference. AMEN

REVELATION CHAPTER 22
20 ¶ He which testifieth these things saith, Surely I come quickly. Amen. Even so, come, Lord JESUS.

(John4:9) (John15:17) John 10:10 The thief cometh not, but for to steal, and to kill, and to destroy: I am come, that they might have life, and that they might have it more abundantly. John 19:30 It is Finished

www.ingramcontent.com/pod-product-compliance
Lightning Source LLC
Chambersburg PA
CBHW061738070526
44585CB00024B/2724